COLLEGE
THE CRUEL JOKE
UNLESS YOU KNOW THE PUNCHLINE!

BRANDICE N. HENDERSON

ENFINITI
PUBLISHING, INC.

Published by:
Enfiniti Publishing Inc.
PO Box 175
New York, NY 10037
www.collegepunchline.com

Contributor/Editor: Kersea Johnson

Editors: Katrinna Bryant, Kimberly Galloway

Copyeditor: Julia Henderson

Proofreader: Todd Hunter, Literary Consultant Group

Book Designer: Adolphus "Danja Mowf" Maples
www.mowfmedia.com

Illustrations: S. Ross Browne

Typesetting: Shawna A. Grundy
sag@shawnagrundy.com

Printed in the United States of America.

ISBN 978-0-9820132-0-5

Table of Contents

Introduction

The Proof is in the Punchline – *Throughout the book, several successful college graduates aka witnesses are interviewed. Their interviews are based on personal experiences of finding a job in their fields after college. I hope that these interviews serve as inspiration, information, and education for the journey that awaits you.*

Dedication

This book is dedicated to Kersea Johnson. Your smile and sense of humor in the midst of suffering has inspired me as well as others to live life to its fullest. I could not have done this without you.

Introduction

I decided to write this book one year after I graduated from college. There I was with a degree and a smile, without a decent job in sight for miles. No, I should say a million miles! At that time, I felt like my college years were a waste of time and energy. I could not believe what a disappointment "the real world" was, and I felt like having a degree meant absolutely nothing.

It seemed that the only asset every employer wanted was *experience*. I realized that I had spent four years working hard to obtain a degree while I should have also spent them gaining the experience that each of my potential employers wanted. No one, and I mean not one single person, including my parents, teachers, or professors had warned me that I would be in such a position. All they ever told me was that one infamous sentence we've all heard at least once in our life: "Go to college so that you can get a good job." They should have just told me to join my high school basketball team so that I would have a future in the WNBA. That seemed more attainable than getting this "good job". My situation felt like a very cruel joke to me.

Fast forward years later and I now realize that the problem was not my degree. The problem was that I had not prepared for the moment after walking across the stage to receive that wonderful degree that I thought was my "ticket" to a great paying job. I spent a great deal of time going to class, writing papers, and studying for tests, but I was not prepared for what was to come after graduation.

The reality is that having a college degree alone is not enough. Being a fresh-college graduate with no relevant work experience made my journey of finding a "good job" extremely difficult. Reflecting back on that time, I now know my biggest mistake: I had not prepared myself for what was to come after I received the degree. In this book, I will coach you on how to successfully get through college, but more importantly, I will provide the information you need to attain a great job in your chosen field. After reading this book, my hope is that you will not repeat the same mistakes so many college graduates do, including myself. After receiving my degree, being frustrated with the lack of job options, regretting the moment I ever went to school, finally working in my field, and living out my dreams, I finally get it ---- The Punchline!!!

GoodBye High School!

HELLO
my name is

College Student

COLLEGE IS FOR EVERYONE
COLLEGE IS FOR EVERYONE
COLLEGE IS FOR EVERYONE
COLLEGE IS FOR EVERYONE
COLLEGE IS FOR EVERYONE
COLLEGE IS FOR EVERYONE

CHAPTER 1

Chapter 1

College Is for Everyone

The title of this book could lead you to believe that college is a waste of time. The truth is that many college graduates feel that college was a cruel joke because they did not have a road map to guide them through their college years. College is actually an experience that could set the stage for a great future.

This book is not meant to discourage anyone from increasing his or her knowledge and creating the invaluable network that only a college experience can provide. If you have the desire to obtain a higher education after high school, college is for you! What's more is that college is not limited to those who want to pursue only traditional professional roles. If you have a unique interest in majors such as music production, film, fashion, photography, art, or whatever your passion may be, that does not fit into the typical "university" curriculum, there is a school for you. There are so many different types of colleges. No one should be left out.

How to Find the Right College:

Here are a few suggestions to follow when searching for a school that is perfect for you:

1. **Search for schools that have majors to fit your interest.** The first step is to know your interest. Take a few moments to jot down the answers to the following questions. What do you enjoy doing? What was your best subject in school? What careers do you find interesting? Once you have identified your passion and interests, the next step is to research several career options that will complement your interests. There are many

people working at jobs and companies that they hate because they chose a profession based on salary or availability instead of pursuing a career they would enjoy. You have a fresh start. Find your true passion and follow it.

2. **Attend the best schools in whatever field you choose.** I attended a school in Tennessee and entered with a pre-med concentration because I was not aware of the many different career options that were available. I definitely had no clue that there were "real" jobs that matched my true passion, fashion. After enrolling in a science course, taking a true assessment of my interest, and speaking with my school counselor, I decided that pre-med was not for me. I changed my major to fashion merchandising.

Besides the fact that my parents were a little upset that I changed my major, the real issue was that I was now at a school that did not specialize in my major. There were only two to three professors in my major that actually worked in the fashion-merchandising field. The remaining professors had never worked in the field. All they could really teach me was book knowledge that I could get by reading on my own. I knew that if I actually had gone to a school whose primary focus was fashion; my experience would have been much more valuable.

If you are confident about your passion and career goals, commit to attending a school that will groom you for a career in that field of study. Your commitment could mean taking risks and making sacrifices, such as moving far from home. Do not let the fear of leaving home, friends, a boyfriend, or girlfriend hold you back from attaining an education that will prepare you for a successful future. The people that are meant to be in your life will be there, no matter how far you go from home. There are many people that never left home because of fear and they now live with regrets about what could have been. This is officially your life. The decisions you make today will affect your tomorrow.

3. **Choose a school that has professors who have worked in**

your field of study. Ask the school advisors if the professors have worked in that field or the percentage of professors that have worked in that field. For example, if you want to major in film, try not to choose a school that has film production professors that have never worked in the film industry. What can they really teach you other than what's in the books? They have no real hands-on knowledge, nor do they have any connections to the industry. If your professors have actually worked in film production, they will probably still have friends that work in the industry. They can give you the benefits and real challenges you will face in the industry that will prepare you for your future. They could also reach out to friends for possible internship opportunities for you. There are so many advantages to being taught by a person who has not only read about it, but has lived it.

4. **Make sure the school you choose is accredited.** Accreditation simply means that the school offers quality education. You can check the accreditation status by going to http://ope.ed.gov/accreditation/.

5. **Visit the college to get a real sense of what college life will be like for you.** Check out the dorms, talk to students, meet professors, and hang out in the cafeteria. This will give you a preview of your college experience at that particular school.

Now that you know all of the qualities to look for in a school, the next step is to actually find the schools that meet your criteria. Here are a few places to look:

1. **The High School Counselor's Office.** This is the first place to start. This office should have a library of information related to college entry. The counselor is usually responsible for helping students with the process of college entry.

2. **College Matchmaking Internet Sites.** A very valuable site that offers "college matchmaking" is http://www.collegeboard.com/student. This site is great because it allows you to type in all of your personal preferences such as: school type, location,

academics, campus life, activities, sports, majors, admission, cost, financial aid, and deadlines. There are many other college matchmaking sites that can be found by using any of the popular search engines.

3. **Internet Search Engines.** Type a major that interest you into a search engine such as Google, Yahoo, or MSN. Several schools will appear that have this major.

After you have found as many schools as possible that have majors that fit your interests, go to each school's website to request an admissions package, or call the admissions office. The phone number is usually found on the school's website under "contact us". The school's information package will usually include all of the admissions information you can find on-line. The information package will include an application, in-depth information on the school, campus, and majors available as well as other information that will try to encourage you to attend that school. Ideally, the process of researching colleges should take place as early as your sophomore year of high school. If you have procrastinated, begin this process as quickly as possible. Be very aware of admissions deadlines. If you need financial assistance, be mindful of financial aid cut-off dates. Searching for the right college can be stressful because of all of the paperwork that must be submitted on time in order to receive admissions or financial aid. However, if you give yourself enough time, it could actually be fun.

Application Process

Most college admissions offices require the following:

- ✓ A Completed Application. This can be filled out on-line or by mail.
- ✓ An Application Fee. Each college will have an application fee. It is important to note that students with financial need can have this fee waived. This is usually determined by students receiving free or reduced lunch, but check with the university for more information.
- ✓ An Official High School Transcript. This can be obtained

from your high school counselor.

✓ ACT and/or SAT Scores. A college may require scores from both tests. Please be sure to carefully check the requirements for each school.

✓ Recommendation Letter(s). A college may require you to submit a recommendation letter from a guidance counselor, the leader of an organization that you are a member of, an employer, or anyone in leadership that is willing to validate your worthiness of attending that particular school. This letter may include your great work ethic, positive attitude, or ambition.

✓ A Personal Statement. You should write one really good personal statement that can be sent to all colleges. Check the specific requirements of each school. You may need to tweak this statement depending on the requirements. This statement gives you the opportunity to sell yourself. A personal statement can be used to explain a deficiency such as a low grade point average due to an illness, family emergency, or any hardship. This letter could be used to display your ability to beat the odds. When writing, mention a specific obstacle you have overcome. It is also important to explain why you have chosen that school and specifically why you are attending college. There are many resources available to assist you with writing a personal statement. Type the words "college personal statements" into a search engine and you will get very detailed tips on how to write an outstanding personal statement.

The points above are only the basic requirements. As the requirements are different for every college, you must check on the university's website to find out their specific requirements. When applying to schools, I suggest using the "notebook method" of organizing the application process. This method is simple and only requires that you purchase a 3-ring binder and dividers. If you are applying to 10 schools, buy enough dividers so that you will have 10 sections in the notebook. It is suggested that you apply to at least 10 schools so that you will have options. This could get expensive with all of the application fees, so be sure to save in advance for this process. In each section of the notebook, write down the name of the school and the requirements for entry. See the following example:

Example:

College or University:_____

Street Address: _____

City, State, Zip Code: _____

Deadline for Admissions: _____

Contact Information:
    Name: _____
    Admissions Phone Number: _____
    Email Address: _____
    Web Address: _____

General Admissions Requirements:
    Application Fee: $_____   Date Sent: _____
    Date High School Transcript Sent: _____
    Essay Required: _____
    Tuition Cost: _____

Additional Admissions Requirements: (F/O = Follow Up)
    1._____ Completion Date: _____ F/O Date: _____
    2._____ Completion Date: _____ F/O Date: _____
    3._____ Completion Date: _____ F/O Date: _____
    4._____ Completion Date: _____ F/O Date: _____

Special Features (Use this section to note special features of the college or university which could be nice dorms, scholarships, or a great location):
    1._____
    2._____
    3._____
    4._____
    5._____

Challenges (Use this section to note undesirable traits of the school, if any):

1._____

2._____

3._____

4._____

5._____

Once you have completed and submitted each requirement, the last step is to call the school to make sure that they have received your completed application. Once it is confirmed that the school has everything they need for your admission, write a big **"COMPLETE"** on the top of that page and wait for your admissions letter.

Taking the SAT (Scholastic Assessment Test) or ACT (previously known as American College Testing)

During the process of finding the school you want to attend, you must also start taking the SAT or ACT college admission exams. The purpose of the SAT and ACT tests are to determine your college readiness. Most colleges require that you take at least one of these exams. Check with the college you plan to attend to find out which exam is required for admissions. Also find out the score needed for admissions. Your goal should be to make the highest score possible on these exams since colleges will use these scores to determine if you are prepared for college level courses. This score may ultimately determine your admissions status.

Here are a few facts about the ACT:

1. The ACT is given 6 times a year: September, October, December, February, April, and June. The test is always given on a Saturday and registration is required about 1 month before the testing date.
2. Scores – The scoring ranges from 1 – 36. Only the correct answers are counted, so it is best not to leave any questions

blank. There is a limited amount of time to complete each section. The test is divided into four sections:

- English   75 Questions *(Sub-scoring - 40 questions Usage/Mechanics, 35 questions Rhetorical Skills)*
- Math   60 Questions *(Sub-scoring - 24 questions pre-algebra, 18 questions intermediate algebra/coordinate geometry, 18 questions plane geometry/trigonometry based)*
- Reading   40 Questions *(Sub-scoring - 20 questions social studies and natural sciences, 20 questions prose fiction and humanities)*
- Science   40 Questions *(no sub-scoring)*
- Writing   Optional Essay Question
  There is a possible score of 36 for each of the four sections. When you receive your scores, check the score for each section to know what areas need improvement.

3. Score Reporting – The ACT will report, at no cost, your scores to the first four schools that you list during ACT registration. After the fourth school, there is a cost per school. If you plan to re-test and you prefer that only your highest score be sent, do not list any schools on the registration form. If you choose this option, you will have to pay to send the scores out to colleges later. The cost is approximately $8.50 per school. Whenever you are ready to have your scores sent to the schools of your choice, you can choose the highest score to be sent.

4. After taking the test, the scores will be available approximately 2 ½ to 3 weeks on-line or 4 to 8 weeks by mail.

5. The current fee for taking the ACT is $30 without the writing portion and $45 with the writing portion. This fee usually increases by a small percentage every year.

6. All fees for the ACT can be waived depending on a student's financial need (usually depends if student is on free or reduced lunch program). The fee waiver form should come from your

school counselor. The website for the ACT with all ACT related information is http://www.actstudent.org or you can call the ACT office using the phone number on the website. This website can be used to find the dates that the test will be given, the locations where the test will be administered, the national average of students across the world, and so much more.

Here are a few facts about the SAT:

1. The SAT is given 6 to 7 times a year. The usual test months are October, November, December, January, March, May, and possibly June. The SAT is available in the United States and Canada as well as other sites around the world.

2. Scores – The scoring ranges from 200 to 800. A partial deduction will be taken for incorrect answers. There is a limited amount of time to complete each section. No deduction is taken for unanswered questions. The SAT is divided into 3 parts:

    -   Math   54 Questions *(44 multiple choice questions and 10 questions that require write-in answers including numbers & operations, algebra & functions, geometry & measurement, data analysis, statistics, & probability)*
    -   Reading   67 Critical Reading/Vocabulary Questions *(19 sentence completion questions and 48 reading comprehension questions)*
    -   Writing   49 Questions and an Essay *(24 questions improving sentences, 18 questions identifying sentence errors, 6 questions improving paragraphs)*

3. Score Reporting - SAT will always report all of your scores to colleges. If after taking the test, you decide that you do not want your scores sent to any schools, ask the test administrator

for a Cancel Test Scores form. The form should be filled out immediately and given to the administrator the same day. Your test will not be scored or reported. Test fees will not be refunded.

4. After taking the test, the scores will be available approximately 3 1/2 weeks on-line or approximately 5 weeks by mail.

5. The current fee for taking the SAT is $45 for the reasoning portion. For subject testing the application cost is $20 plus $9 for each subject. Every college has different requirements. If a school requires the SAT, check to see if they have any subject requirements. The fee may change each year, so check the website for the most up-to-date information.

6. Some of the fees for the SAT can be waived depending on a student's financial need (usually depends if student is on free or reduced lunch program). The fee waiver form should come from your school's counselor.

7. The website for the SAT with all SAT related information is http://www.collegeboard.com, or you can call this office using the phone number on the website. This website can be used to find the dates that the test will be given, the locations where the test will be administered, the national average of students across the world, and so much more.

For more information and tips about college readiness tests, I consulted with Mrs. Louella Bailey, an SAT coach for 15 years and educator for 32 years. When I asked Mrs. Bailey the best way for students to prepare for college readiness tests such as the ACT and SAT, she said, "Start early. Learn everything that you can in your daily classes. There is no substitute for a good knowledge base. Students should always read. Remember the adage, *readers rule the world.* Two-thirds of the test depends on your vocabulary and how extensively you have read. Reading must extend beyond the classroom assignments. It must include newspapers, magazines, outside books and yes -- no matter your religion -- the Bible." In regards to preparation for the test, Mrs. Bailey offers the following comments: "By the time a student enters freshman year, 9th grade, he or she should begin to hone their skills by participating in test preparation classes. Most high schools have free classes. See your school's guidance counselor to learn more about these programs. For students who take a professional course, these courses should be completed by the spring of their junior year." Mrs. Bailey offers several tips for taking the SAT and ACT:

- ✓ Keep a vocabulary file on index cards. Add to and review this file regularly.
- ✓ Take practice test periodically. Time and score yourself.
- ✓ Use any of the popular study guides such as: Princeton Review, Barrons, Kaplan's, etc. All are good.
- ✓ Free practice tests are available on-line. Practicing the test on the computer is good for becoming accustomed to the types of questions that will be on the SAT; however, sitting down for paper and pencil practice tests truly acclimates you for the test because it mimics the experience you will have.
- ✓ In order to score well in writing, students must be able to express their thoughts with articulation. You must be able to develop a particular topic and reinforce it with information from the past or with statistical data. If you can bring in a book or article to support your points, you should score well on the writing section.
- ✓ Preliminary Scholastic Aptitude Test (PSAT) should be taken the fall of your 10th and 11th grade year.
- ✓ Taking the PSAT is most important for minority students that wish to attend college. Colleges begin to take notice of students who do well on the PSAT as early as in their sophomore year (10th grade). Juniors that score in the 90 percentile or higher -- which means that a student has scored better than 90% of other juniors -- are ensured financial assistance if they validate this score with a comparable SAT score. National Achievement Scholarships are based on PSAT scores.

It is important to review the SAT and ACT websites for the most up-to-date information regarding test dates, fees, and locations administering the tests. Free practice tests are available on the website for the ACT (http://www.actstudent.org) and SAT (http://www.collegeboard.com) as well as other sites such as www.number2.com.

I was not accepted.

The word "no" is a very short word. It doesn't offer much explanation nor does it have an eloquent sound to it. It's simply a two-letter word that contains much power for some and very little power for others. For extremely successful people such as Donald Trump, Russell Simmons, and Oprah, I could only assume that the word "no" has little meaning. When this two-letter word comes knocking at your door, you have two choices: 1) accept it with open arms, hug it, nurture it, and get real cozy with it, or 2) make it wait at the door while you do whatever you have to do (ethically of course) to get "yes" to come over and smash "no". Do you think that Russell Simmons cozies up with "no"? How often do you think Donald Trump has been turned down for loans for his extravagant projects? "No" is a word you will hear many times throughout your life. "Did I get the job?" No. "Was I approved for the loan?" No. "Did I get accepted into any of the schools I applied to?" No. That last "no" could be devastating for a high school senior. Maybe your grade point average and test scores on the ACT or SAT did not meet the admissions requirement. Whatever the reason, the real issue is what you plan to do with this "no".

My nephew taught me a powerful saying that we would chant as we approached what seemed like an impossible hill during one of our many summer bike rides: "Winners find a way; losers make excuses." This simple chant got us up and over the hill. The best reply to the answer "no" is, "I'll find a way." If you find yourself in a situation where you have not been admitted to any four-year university, your first step is to write a letter to the dean of admissions. In this letter express your reason for wanting to attend college and that school in particular. Be as sincere and convincing as possible. Admit your mistakes -- which could include that you did not work to your full potential in high school -- but most importantly, give specific examples of how you plan to succeed in college. If there were situations that happened beyond your control that affected your grade point average such as a serious illness, a death of a loved one, or abuse, include this in your letter. Be sure to address the letter with the dean of admissions' full name and not "Admissions Office". After checking for grammatical mistakes, be sure that your contact information is in the letter. Once you send the letter to the Admissions Office, follow up within a week. It may take ten calls before you can speak to someone, but persistence is key to your success in college. In addition to sending the letter and following up on it, set up an appointment to speak with the admissions counselor. You will need to sell yourself at this meeting. In your face-to-face meeting, arrive as you would for an interview. I suggest that you skip to Chapter 12 for instructions on how to present yourself on an interview.

If you are still not admitted after you have followed up on your letter and have met with an admissions advisor in person, don't fret. There is another solution! Temporarily attend a two-year *accredited* junior college and after two years, transfer to a four-year university. I know several people who took this route and they are very successful. Don't waste your time complaining about not attending a big university. Take this time to study, get focused, and then transfer. Before deciding what classes to take at the 2-year college, set up an appointment with an admissions counselor at the four-year university of your choice. Find out which classes will transfer to the four-year university. ***DO NOT ENROLL IN CLASSES THAT WILL NOT TRANSFER TO YOUR FUTURE UNIVERSITY.*** There is nothing worse than wasting time and money taking courses that will not transfer. When visiting the university to speak with an admissions counselor, do not leave until you speak to someone. It is not always easy to get quick answers at any university. You must be persistent enough to keep going until you get an answer, patient enough to wait in long lines, and assertive enough to sell yourself to the admissions counselor.

The process of college entrance should take place during your junior year of high school but no later than the 1st semester of your senior year. Many students wait until the last minute to start researching scholarships and colleges, but if you wait too long, you could miss extremely urgent deadlines. The process of college admissions is a tedious process that takes a great deal of preparation, but the results are well worth it.

The Proof is in the Punchline

Witness #1: Rashida Maples

Who is your current employer?
- A law firm

What is your title?
- Attorney

What was your major in college?
- Business Administration and Law

Why did you choose this major?
- I always wanted a nice office, nice paycheck, and something that essentially put me in charge of everything
- Regarding law, I wanted to work in the entertainment industry and felt that the legal industry was the most stable area to be in.

What advice would you give a college student concerning finding a job after college, choosing a major, or preparing for the real world?
- Attend college and/or graduate school in whatever city or area you want to work in. If a certain city or state is where your industry is booming, go there immediately... while you're still in school. Push fear to the side, and just go for what you want.

What general life advice would you give a college student?
- Have fun, but definitely talk to people who are where you want to be. They can give you advice on the ropes to skip and the ropes to jump through. Also, it's so cliché, but anything worth having is going to take time. Always go for your goals.

CHAPTER 2

Chapter 2

Paying for College

What do you do if your grades are on point, your test scores are acceptable, but you have no money to cover college tuition? Expenses can range from $1,500 to $20,000 a semester, depending on the college you choose. Affording college is a hurdle that is easy to jump with preparation and planning. If you lack the funds to cover tuition, there are three solutions: scholarships, grants, or student loans. Scholarships are financial awards that do not have to be paid back, but they do have special requirements that are set by the organization, company, or person providing the financial award. A grant is free money provided by the government for college tuition based on need. Student loans are provided to students for tuition, but must be paid back. The process of finding money for college should ideally start the end of your junior year. If you are a senior and have not started this process, do not procrastinate any longer.

The preferred method of funding your tuition is by obtaining free money in the form of scholarships. Every college bound student should apply for scholarships regardless of tuition need. Scholarships are provided based on criteria set by the provider. The criteria could be based on your ethnic background, GPA, financial need, music abilities, athletics, your parents' civic involvement, etc. There are thousands of scholarships available provided by many different sources including colleges, corporations, individuals, the government, religious organizations, and many more. Scholarships can be found by checking with your school counselor or the financial aid office of the schools you've applied to. Another great place to look is the Internet of course. The government actually offers information on different scholarships available by visiting the following website www.studentaid.ed.gov. Click on "Financial Aid and Scholarship Wizard" and then go to "Search for Scholarships". There are also several other independent sites such as www.fastweb.com that offer in-depth information on scholarships available to high school seniors. Scholarship websites can be found by typing in keywords such as "academic scholarships" into a search engine. These sites will usually ask approximately 30 personal questions such as your name, school interests, grade point average, test scores, etc. Once you enter all of your information, the website will provide you with scholarship matches based on the criteria that you meet. The deadlines, amounts of the scholarship, and the requirements to receive each scholarship will be listed. There may be additional responsibilities to send requested information such as essays, projects, videos, etc. Because of the many different requirements needed for every scholarship, it is important that you stay organized. As with college applications, the notebook system is also perfect for organizing the scholarship application process. Again, buy a 3-ring notebook, dividers, and folders that can go into the notebook. Divide the notebook into sections for each scholarship, print out the requirements and contact information to place in the folder of that section, list the requirements, and mark them off once each requirement is completed.

Example:

Scholarship: _____

Deadline for Submission: _____

Contact Information:

      Name: _____

      Phone Number:_____ _____

      Email Address: _____

      Web Address: _____

Requirements:

      1._____

      Completion Date: _____ Follow Up Date: _____

      2._____

      Completion Date: _____ Follow Up Date: _____

      3._____

      Completion Date: _____ Follow Up Date: _____

      4._____

      Completion Date: _____ Follow Up Date: _____

Once you have submitted all necessary information to obtain the scholarship, write a big **"COMPLETE"** on the page. If possible, follow up with the scholarship provider to make sure that they received all of your information. The process of applying for scholarships will require extra time and effort on your part, but it is worth it to receive free money for college, books, or dorm fees. Maybe you'll receive so much money that you can buy items for your dorm room. If someone stood in front of you with a thousand dollars, you would definitely go through a few hoops to get this money. It's the same for scholarships. It's free money! I suggest that you apply for at least 20 scholarships. Start the process of searching and applying for scholarships no later than the 1st month of your senior year, though it is best to start even sooner. Lastly, it is important to note that you will receive plenty of junk email when providing your information to scholarship websites, so I suggest creating a special email account to receive college information only.

In addition to scholarships, other ways to fund your college tuition is by applying for grants or loans. In order to receive a grant or loan, you must go to www.fafsa.ed.gov and complete the application for financial aid. The application for financial aid is available on this free website. The form is usually available in January for the next school year. For example, if you are applying for the 2011/2012 school year, the financial aid form will be available on-line January 2011. This website offers any information or instructions needed on how to apply for financial aid. If you have any questions after reading through the website, you should call the financial aid office. The phone number is available on the site under "contact us". You should never pay any person or website for assistance with applying for financial aid because the government offers so much free help with this process. The financial aid application may be filled out on-line or you may fill out a hard copy to be mailed. The on-line applications are processed quicker than the hard copies. If you prefer a hard copy, they can usually be found in university financial aid offices, libraries, or with your school counselor. The most important information you will need for these forms is your parents' or guardians' current income tax information. This is the information that will determine your eligibility for grants and loans based on need. If you are independent, this form will require your income tax information. It is important to note that financial aid can be obtained for any school that has a federal ID code. This includes beauty and barber schools, technical colleges, mechanical schools, and more. You can check to see if a school has a federal ID code by going to http://www.fafsa.ed. Click on "search for school codes". If you do not see the college you would like to attend, call the FAFSA (Free Application for Federal Student Aid) office to double check the status of a school's federal code.

We will now explore the different grant options available. Please see the following chart:

Figure 2-1

Grant Type	Brief Description	How Much?	Eligibility	Special Notes
Federal Pell Grant	The main, basic form of grants awarded by the government based on financial need and the cost of the school. This is the foundation grant. All other grants will be in addition to the Pell Grant.	The maximum for a year $4,310 (the maxi-mum can change each award year depending on government program funding).	Awarded to undergraduates that have not earned a Bachelor's or professional degree. Based on financial need.	This grant may also be awarded based on the cost of the school you are attending.
Federal Supplemental Educational Opportunity Grant(FSEOG)	Program for undergraduates with exceptional financial needed. Pell Grant recipients with the lowest family contribution will be considered as a priority for this grant.	$100 to $4,000 a year depending on financial need, when you apply, and school policies	Based on severe financial need.	
Academic Competitiveness Grant	This award is granted in addition to the Pell Grant for students that successfully completed a "rigorous high school program". This grant is only available your 1st and 2nd year of college.	$750 max for 1st year, $1300 max for 2nd year.	Students must have a 3.0 from a school with rigorous high school program. US Citizen; Federal Pell Grant Recipient; Enrolled full time in degree program; Enrolled in the first or second academic year of his or her program of study at a 2 year or 4 year accredited college; Not previously enrolled in undergraduate program; If 2nd year student, must have 3.0 GPA on 4.0 scale.	You will not receive this grant if the Pell Grant covers your tuition. This grant is only given to students with additional financial need for tuition even after receiving a Pell Grant. Please go to the following link to find out if your school has a "rigorous program": http://www.ed.gov/about/offices/list/ope/ac-smart.html

The National Science & Mathematics Access to Retain Talent Grant (National SMART Grant)	Available during 3rd and 4th years of undergraduate study to full time students who are eligible for the Pell Grant	Up to $4,000 per year of 3rd or 4th year.	Must be eligible for Pell Grant; US Citizen; Enrolled full-time; 3rd or 4th year students; Majoring in physical, life or computer sciences, mathematics, technology, engineering, or foreign language determined critical to national security; must have 3.0 GPA on 4.0 scale; enrolled at accredited college or university.	Go to the following link for complete list of eligible majors: http://ifap.ed.gov/dpcletters/attachments/Co mpleteListEligibleMajors0708SMART.pdf
Institutional Grants	Provided by some colleges to help make up the difference between college costs and what a family can be expected to contribute. Also known as merit awards.	Varies depending on the college.	Depends on the college requirements.	You will need to check with the college financial aid office to see if these grants/merit awards are available at that particular university. They are some times listed on the college's website.

Reference: U.S. Department of Education, Federal Student Aid, Students Channel, *Funding Education Beyond High School: The Guide to Federal Student Aid 2007-08*, Washington, D.C.

Go To: http://studentaid.ed.gov/students/publications/student_guide/2007-2008/english/loanrepayment.htm for more information

For more information on government grants go to www.ed.gov. There are also grants that are awarded at the state level to residents, so if you plan to attend school in your current state, research grants your state has to offer. One way to find these grants is by using search engines and typing in "your state" and the phrase "educational college grants". You could also ask your high school counselor or the financial aid office of the school you're trying to attend in your state.

Student loans are available to students that are not eligible for grants because of the lack of need, as well as students that still need financial assistance even after receiving scholarships and grants. If at all possible, make loans your last choice. To receive a loan, remember you **must** first fill out a financial aid application. So, what types of student loans are available? There are many different types of student loans and they are not all created equal! Please see figure 2-2:

Figure 2-2

Loan Type	Need vs Non-Need Based	Characteristics	Re-Payment	Special Notes
Stafford	Need-Based	Interest paid by government when student is in school (at least half-time) and during periods of grace and deferment.	Re-payments begin six months after student graduates, withdraw, or attend school less than half-time.	Go To: http://studentaid.ed.gov for the most up to date interest rates
Unsubsidized Stafford	Need-Based	Interest NOT paid by government when student is in school (at least half-time) and during periods of grace and deferment.	Re-payments begin six months after student graduates, withdraw, or attend school less than half-time.	Go To: http://studentaid.ed.gov for the most up to date interest rates
PLUS	Non-Need Based	Enables parents to borrow to pay the costs of higher education for their dependent undergraduates who are enrolled at least half-time; also available to graduate and professional degree students.	60 days after the loan is released from the lender. This means the loan must be paid while the undergraduate student is in school.	Go To: http://studentaid.ed.gov for the most up to date interest rates
Federal Perkins Loan	Need-Based	Interest paid by government when student is in school and during periods of grace and deferment.	Nine months after student graduates, withdraws, or attends school less than half time.	Borrowers who undertake certain public, military, or teaching service employment are eligible to have all or part of their loans cancelled.

Reference: U.S. Department of Education, Federal Student Aid, Students Channel, *Funding Education Beyond High School: The Guide to Federal Student Aid 2007-08*, Washington, D.C.
Go To: http://studentaid.ed.gov/students/publications/student_guide/2007-2008/english/loanrepayment.htm for more information

Stafford and Perkins Loans are preferred because the government pays the interest on the loan while you are in school. The Perkins Loan can actually be cancelled if you graduate and work in certain service fields such as military or education. In addition to federal loans, there are also private loans available, but they usually come with a higher interest rate. Please be smart and attentive of interest rates. They may not seem to be important now, but they will be later.

Many people view student loans negatively. If student loans are borrowed wisely, they should be considered a great investment. If you need a loan to finance your college education because you do not qualify for any grants or scholarships, it is an investment well worth it. The following are benefits student loans offer:

o   Student loans carry a much lower interest rate than normal loans.

o   The bank will give you approximately six months to find a job after graduation. Afterwards, payments on your loan will be due unless you are enrolled in school or become permanently disabled.

o   There are 2 options if a student is not able to make repayments: forbearance or deferment. These options are granted to college graduates that are unemployed, experiencing economic hardship, currently enrolled in school or become disabled. A forbearance allows a graduate to postpone their student loan; however, the interest continues to accrue for all loans during this period. A forbearance is usually granted for a time period of 12 months. A deferment is similar; however, the interest does not accrue during a deferment for the Perkins and Subsidized Stafford Loans. The time period for a deferment is usually longer than forbearance. If you apply for either of these, you must continue making payments until you have received notice that a forbearance or deferment is approved. To apply for these options the graduate must contact the lender.

Many of us have heard the age-old stories of the never-ending saga of student loans and the debt they can cause. Well, unfortunately, this is not a myth. Student loans can become extremely difficult to pay back for the following reasons:

1. **A student drops out of college and is not able to afford to make payments on the loan.** If you take out a student loan and drop out of college, your payments are due immediately. Payment plans can be made if the lender is contacted for an arrangement.

2. **A student decides not to make loan payments.** If a loan cannot be paid back due to financial difficulty, an arrangement must be made with the lender as soon as possible. If an arrangement is not made, the loan will go into default. A defaulted student loan has many consequences including possible garnishment of your paycheck or income tax return. It will also affect your credit negatively which will affect your ability to get an apartment, car, credit card or even a job since many employers now run a credit check before making a hiring decision. The government will not allow a student to take out any new loans if they have a defaulted loan.

3. **A student borrows more money than what is needed for tuition expenses.** The more you borrow, the more you must pay back. The banks will offer more loan money as you increase your years in college. Do not take out any extra loan money unless it is needed. Taking out extra money will only prolong the time it takes to repay the loan. It may seem like free money, but it's not!

The worst mistake students make is not calling the lender when they are unable to make payments. This was my situation. I could not afford to make student loan payments shortly after graduation, so I decided not to pay my loans. My loans went into default and this decision affected my credit for years! I finally entered a loan rehabilitation program and got my loans out of default by making fourteen monthly payments on time. **NOT PAYING YOUR LOANS**

WILL SERIOUSLY RUIN YOUR CREDIT!

If you are still not clear about your financial options, please visit the financial aid office of the school you want to attend. Most of us do not have the money to pay outright for college tuition; therefore, the financial aid office is always busy. Be prepared to sacrifice hours to speak with an advisor one-on-one and have your questions already prepared.

Besides student loans, there is one other debt that students fall prey to that is not considered an investment, but a liability: Credit Cards. As soon as you enter college, companies will begin sending you credit card applications. There will be companies that will come to your school's campus offering gifts and perks to sign up for this debt with interest and it will not matter to them if you have a job or not. It will be tempting, but do not apply for credit cards. When you charge something you will pay for it now or later. I had to spend my graduation money to pay off credit card bills. This is avoidable debt. Please understand that if you do not pay your credit card bills it will ruin your credit.

Please make this vow: "I will not take out any unnecessary student loans because I will have to pay them back. If I cannot make payments on my student loan, I will call the lender to make necessary payment arrangements."

The Proof is in the Punchline

Witness #2: Kenia Valentin

Who is your current employer?
- Narco Freedom, Inc. – A non-profit multi-service agency in NYC.

What is your title?
- Quality Assurance Specialist – I am part of a team that is responsible for ensuring that all of the agency's programs are in compliance with New York State licensing requirements.

What was your major in college?
- Social Work

What was your first job out of college?
- I worked at University Settlement House. It's a community services agency in the Lower East Side of Manhattan. I worked in the Entitlements Department. I assisted mainly Spanish only speaking clients in applying for public assistance, housing, reading documents for them, preparing them for appointments etc.

How did you get this job? Are you happy with your career?
- I went to one of the best social work schools in NY, NYU. The school sets up internships for every social work student for their junior or senior years. I interned there and was offered a position upon graduation.
- I am happy with my career, and am looking forward to where it takes me!

What advice would you give a college student concerning finding a job after college, how to choose a major, or any subject related?
- If you're not sure what you want to major in, I suggest going to a large university and taking classes in a few areas that you find interesting. Don't rush to declare a major. Wait until your junior year. Ask everyone you know for contacts in the fields that interests you. Look them up, meet with them. People enjoy talking about what they do and love it if you're willing to volunteer. Be proactive.
- Look for all the assistance that is available to you. I remember feeling a little ashamed about asking for job study opportunities or financial aid. Research and push for whatever help you can receive to get you through college and graduate.

- If you do know what career you want to pursue, strive to attend one of the best schools for that field.

What general life advice would you give a college student?

- College can be a really hard time in your life. It's a transition time from adolescence to adulthood. Create a community for yourself in school. A community of people who have your best interest at heart. This is very important, especially if you're the only student from your high school going to that college or you are transitioning from a small high school to a large university.
- College can provide great opportunities for new experiences, step out of your comfort zone. Try out for a team, join a club/organization, and take a fun/crazy class. Do a semester abroad. Enjoy this time of exploration before you have to get focused on a career path.
- Find out what the salary ranges are for the career you want to pursue. It can be a rude awakening. It's important to make informed choices regarding your career while considering the lifestyle you want to have.

A Special Note to High School Graduates

Congratulations! You managed to make it home after the prom in one piece. You held back the tears as they called your best friend's name at graduation. You spent hours writing essays and filling out college applications. You've taken the SAT and/or ACT, completed financial aid papers, and have been accepted into a university. You can finally exhale! You made it through the summer and you're here as a freshman in college. You have probably already screamed, "I'M FREE!!! No mom. No dad. No teachers. There is no one to tell me what time to come in, what to do, when to do it, or how to do it. I can go out and come in at anytime I please. I can make my own decisions without anyone asking me any questions." Maybe you're not feeling this way, but this was exactly how I felt. I had been 18 for five months but never truly felt like an adult until my parents dropped me off at college for the first time. All I could think about, besides finally being my own boss, was all the fun I was about to have. College life can be loads of fun, but the reality is that college is survival of the fittest. This is why so many students decide to drop out. Be sure not to get so caught up in the hype of college life that you forget about the time and effort it will take to graduate.

Being accepted into a university and becoming a college student are great accomplishments. Because of the tedious, time consuming effort it takes to go through the process of college admissions, many high school graduates forego college. So again, congratulations! You did it and everyone is proud of you!

Now that you've given yourself a big pat on the back, it's time to get down to business!

I'm in!
Now What?

Dear College Applicant:

We are happy to inform you that your application to our four year institution has been has been accepted and you have been awarded a four year scholarship. Now your life really begins. Do you have any idea what your major will be? Do you even know why you applied to College? We're happy to inform you that no one will be watching over you making sure that you complete your work or even go to class.

You have hopefully left your mother at home so now you really have to be responsible for yourself and all that your future holds. This is really make it or break it time, so don't take it lightly. If you have any questions, you can be sure to have to find the answers for yourself because just like real life, nothing will come easy here.

So congratulations, and good luck... you're going to need it.

Sincerely,
Dean Mean
Hello College

CHAPTER 3

Chapter 3

Choosing Classes and Credit Hours

College offers you the privilege of choosing what classes you want to take and when you want to take them. Your responsibility is to make sure that the classes you choose are the classes you will need to graduate. All colleges have academic advisors that will assist you in choosing your classes. (Meeting with an academic advisor usually only requires making an appointment to meet with them.) Before registering, you should be prepared with answers to the following questions:

1. How many classes should you take?

In order to discuss this point, you should first know how many credit hours are required to graduate in your major. This information can be found by looking in your academic catalog, on the school's website, or visiting the academic advisor's office. Once you have this number, divide it by the number of years required to complete that major. This will give you the number of credit hours you must take per year. For example, if your degree only requires four years and a total of 120 hours it would take about 30 credit hours per academic year. If you attend a school that has a two semester year, it would calculate to an average of 15 credit hours per semester to graduate. If you are pursuing a bachelor's degree, keep in mind that some majors require four years, while other majors could require five. Once you know how many credit hours you need to take per semester, the next step is to find out the category each class falls under. See the following example:

EXAMPLE:

Bachelor's Degree [1]
Total Hours to Graduate: 120 Credit Hours
General Education Classes: 45 Credit Hours
Major-oriented courses: 69 Credit Hours
Electives: 6 Credit Hours

2. What classes should you take?

Now that you know how many hours you should take on average per semester, the next step is to decide what classes to take. For freshmen, I have one major rule: Set yourself up for success!

Your first semester is a big adjustment period. You are learning how to budget money, live with roommates, make decisions independent from your parents and more. Adjusting to college life can be really tough. If a difficult course load is added to this adjustment period, it can be extremely stressful. The following are suggestions to consider before you decide what classes to take:

- **Choose subjects that you are strong in and not classes that will be difficult:** If you know that math is a struggle for you, do not take calculus your first semester. However, if you are a math person you may want to choose Algebra or another general math course if it's required for your major.
- **Choose enough classes to drop one, if necessary.** If you only want to take 12 hours, sign up for 15. This will allow you to drop one class in case you are struggling later. There is usually a one to two week grace period to drop a class without penalty. If the course is dropped within the grace period, you will usually receive a full refund for this dropped course. On your transcript the course will not appear for that semester and it will seem as if you never registered for the course.

In order to drop a course, most colleges require that you write a letter or fill out a drop class form on-line or in person. After the grace

---

1 Since this is only an example, be certain to check your school's course catalog for graduation requirements in this and other areas of study, as graduation requirements vary among schools.

period, you will have to "withdraw" from a class. Withdrawing from a course could cause financial penalties as well as require permission or approval from the department head. It is much wiser to drop a course. This usually requires no approval or permission forms.

- **Choose one class that doesn't require much studying in the first semester**. This class usually has a pass or fail grade. These classes are usually some type of physical fitness class. This class may not be easy depending on your fitness level. The great thing about these classes is that most likely if you show up and participate, you'll receive an A.
- **Choose a realistic schedule that is comfortable for you.** If you're not a morning person, don't sign up to take 8:00 a.m. classes. Instead, take classes that start by 9:00 a.m. or maybe even 10:00 a.m. The same rule applies to evening courses. If you're in school full time, without a job, try not to schedule evening courses. Because most students take classes during the day, the evening is usually the time to socialize if you're living on a college campus. It can sometimes be very difficult to break away from your social time to go to class.

The following is an example of a first semester freshman's ideal schedule:

Class 1 – Freshman English (3 hours)
Class 2 – Psychology or Sociology (3 hours)
Class 3 – Freshman Seminar or an Introduction to
          "your major" course (3 hours)
Class 4 – Physical Education (3 hours)
Class 5 – Your choice (elective) (3 hours)

Class 1 – Freshman English: Freshmen are usually required to take English as a general education course. This class may not be easy. It will require that you write several papers and it may take time to adjust to college level writing requirements. Take your grades as constructive criticism. If you struggle with this class, or any class, be assertive by scheduling a meeting with the professor to discuss ways in which you can improve your writing skills. Most English professors realize that college-level writing may be a struggle for most college freshmen and they are usually willing to take extra time to work with you.

Class 2 – Psychology or Sociology: If you enjoy class discussions, these classes can be fun. Psychology and Sociology classes usually aren't extremely difficult, but they do require ample amounts of thinking and reading. These classes may be required for your major, but if not, check to see if it can be used as an elective.

Class 3 – Freshman Seminar or Intro to "your major": If there is a freshman seminar class available at the college you attend, take it. This course helps with the huge adjustment to college life and it is a great way to get to meet new people. It's usually a fairly light course unless you have a professor that decides to make it a difficult course. Introduction classes to your major are normally very interesting and in most cases, these classes are not too difficult.

Class 4 – P.E. This is the class that doesn't require much brainwork. It mostly requires physical work for one hour out of your day. Again, your grade will strongly depend on your attendance, participation, and sometimes fairly easy written tests. There are some P.E. courses that actually require papers and projects. With a little studying these can be passed with ease.

Class 5 – Elective (your choice): Elective courses at most schools can be any course you choose; however, some majors require that you take electives specific to your major. Check your course catalog for this information. If possible, choose an enjoyable elective course, but be careful to avoid classes such as art or music. Don't assume they will be easy A's. Unless you're an art or music major, these classes can be difficult. Art and music classes in college require a large amount of studying, projects, and homework. I remember taking an art course thinking it would be easy. After the professor assigned several projects to complete, using devices I never worked with, such as x-acto pens[2],

---

2 An x-acto pen is sharp knife used in the form of a pen that offers precise cutting and trimming. This tool is often used in art classes.

I quickly realized that I had made a big mistake.

The schedule above is only an example and should be used only as a guide for setting up your schedule for the freshman year. If you only want to take 12 hours, the example above even gives you enough options to drop one class. However, if you want to take 15 hours, you should sign up for 18. Just remember to drop the class before the school's drop deadline, the last date for you to drop a class without a fee. This date can be found in your school calendar.

3. Do the courses you need have prerequisites?
When registering for classes, you should be aware that some classes have prerequisites that are requirements that must be fulfilled before you can take a particular course. A prerequisite could be a lower level course such as Spanish 1 that must be taken before a Spanish 2 course. Another example is a class that requires you to be at a certain class level such as a sophomore. A prerequisite could also be a class that requires a particular grade in a lower level course or a certain score on the ACT, SAT, or placement tests.

Placement tests are given to determine your skill level in certain subjects. The score you make on this test will determine which level of a particular course you may take during your first semester. Math classes usually require that a placement test is taken, unless you are a student that has met the score requirement on the Advanced Placement[3] (AP) exam or the math section of the ACT or SAT. If your score on the placement exam does not meet the required score set by the college to take college-level courses, a remedial course may be required. For example, if a math score of 41 or higher is required on a placement test and your score is 30, a remedial course would be required.

Remedial courses are simply courses that prepare you for college-level courses in a certain subject. Since remedial classes are only preparation classes, earned credit hours are not given for these courses in most cases. See your college advisor or the college website to find

3 Advance Placement classes are advanced classes taught on a college level in high school. At the end of the class, a student may take an AP exam. The AP exam is scored from one to five. Depending on your score, a college may choose to give you college credits for this course. Colleges decide at their discretion what score will qualify a student to receive college credit.

out what courses require a placement test and the score needed to pass the placement test. Also, check the score needed on AP exams, as well as the ACT and SAT that may exempt you from taking any placement tests. If a class requires a prerequisite, the prerequisite will be listed in your school's course catalog or on the school's website.

4. How will you set your class schedule?

Once you know all of the information in steps 1 – 3, you can begin to register for classes. Registration is usually available on-line and is fairly easy. You choose your class and the times this class is offered will be provided to you. Unfortunately, freshmen do not have much flexibility in choosing class times because many classes are already full by the time freshman register. As upperclassmen are allowed to pre-register, classes fill up fast. Once they are closed, you can no longer register for these classes unless you receive signed permission from the department head at most schools. The good news is that as a freshman you are starting at zero credit hours earned, which means you have many options of classes to take.

Some classes will meet a few times a week for approximately 1 hour; other classes meet in the evening once or twice a week for about three hours. If many of the classes you choose are open, registration will be a great experience because you can decide how your days will be set up based on your class schedule. So, if you decide that you want Fridays to be your day of rest, you can simply not register for classes that meet on that day. This option may become more realistic your 2nd semester when you are able to pre-register.

Again, if possible, remember to schedule a comfortable course schedule. As I stated in question #2, if you are not a morning person try not to schedule 8:00 a.m. courses. Also, be sure to use the guide I provided in question #2 above to help you with choosing your classes when registering.

The Proof is in the Punchline

Witness #3: Shani Armstrong

Who is your current employer?
- A non-profit healthcare organization

What is your title?
- Medical Director

What was your major in college?
- Biology

How did you get your current job? Explain your career path.
- I always thought I wanted to be a pediatrician. I went to college and took the MCATS. I was accepted into medical school and then residency. After finishing residency, I wanted to do something other than practice medicine, but it was a big transition since all my experience was solely in clinical medicine. I decided to begin my career in clinical medicine to see if I would change my mind about what I really wanted to do. After joining this organization, I happened to mention to my immediate boss that I was initially interested in doing something other than solely practicing medicine. About two months later (five months into this new job), a project/opportunity for the organization arose and I was offered the position of Medical Director.

What was your first job out of college? How did you get this job?
- All of my previous college summer jobs were related to healthcare. They were set up through a program at the medical school in my hometown for minorities who were interested in medicine. My first summer job was shadowing a radiologist for a month and then shadowing a cardiologist and doing research with him for a month.

What advice would you give a college student concerning finding a job after choosing a major, or preparing for the real world?
- Think about your true long-term goals and what type of lifestyle you'd like to have. Don't just consider the financial aspect of it. There are a multitude of things that you should consider:
   *Think about the time it takes to get the degree that's necessary for your career.
   *Consider the finances necessary to either get the degree or that can be made in the process of getting the degree.
   *The type of schedule you'll have including hours worked on a daily and yearly basis (a 9 month job as a teacher versus a 12 month job) will be an important factor.

       *Consider whether you have control over your schedule or will you always have to work for someone else who sets your schedule.

       *Ask yourself is this career the one that you've always thought you'd have and the one that will make you really happy?

       *Are there location limitations to your career? Are you a California girl and the only place to really perform your career is in a niche market in New York or London?

What general life advice would you give a college student?

- Don't be afraid of the unknown. If you don't know how to do something or how to get to a certain career point or if a certain career endpoint is viable, ASK, ASK, ASK, and ASK more questions. You'll never know if you don't ask. The more people you ask, the better position you'll be in to get what you want out of life. The person that you least expect could be the connection you've been waiting for. Also don't be afraid to meet people and make connections. You never know who that other person knows, what their professional expertise is, or what secret hobby they have. It could mean the difference between you achieving your goals or not.

CHAPTER 4

Chapter 4

Difficult Classes and Professors

As if adjusting to your first year of college isn't difficult enough, there will be professors and classes there to test your perseverance. These classes may cause you to cry, stay up overnight studying, or even make you feel like giving up. It's okay! We've all been there. Difficult classes or professors are a challenge that you will face at some point in your college life, and it's up to you how you will handle it. Sometimes you may encounter a double whammy: both a difficult class and a difficult professor. In this section I will guide you on how to handle the four class combinations that you could face:

1. **Easy Class: Easy Professor**
2. **Easy Class: Hard Professor**
3. **Hard Class: Easy Professor**
4. **Hard Class: Hard Professor**

Before we proceed, let's first look at the definitions:

Easy Class – A class that can be passed with an A or a B with a reasonable amount of studying. Reasonable amount of studying will be defined as two hours a week, which could be broken up to 30 minute study sessions 4 days a week. This class will usually have few assignments, projects, and quizzes. The material covered in this class will be easy for you to learn or may be already familiar to you.

Hard Class – A class that you may struggle in because the lesson is unfamiliar and the material is difficult for you to understand. This class may require many assignments, have difficult exams, or require many projects.

Easy Professor – A professor that is known to give out A's to students that put forth effort. This professor is the kind of teacher that explains the lesson in simple terms, gives extra credit opportunities, takes time to answer or explain any of your questions, and they may drop your lowest quiz score. This professor may be more understanding if you need an extension on an assignment.

Hard Professor – A professor that teaches the lessons in a very difficult manner. This professor may be known to give very few, if any A's to students. He or she is usually not willing to explain and re-explain the material until you understand. This professor may be very demanding with tough assignments, have low tolerance for late assignments, and very strict attendance rules.

Class Combinations

Easy Class: Easy Professor - If you've got an easy class and an easy professor, fortunately, you are in great shape. You won't run into this situation very often. Take advantage of this situation by continuing to do your best. Aim at getting an A. Not even an easy professor is going to give an unearned A, so try your best in these classes.

   If at all possible, you should schedule at least one of these classes a semester. This combination helps even out the stress of your other classes. Your best resource in choosing these classes is upperclassmen. You must be willing to reach out to other students. When I was in school, I would always call around to find out the easiest professors. This is how I would find professors that were fun, let the class go early, gave easy assignments, or had a relaxed attendance policy.

Easy Class: Difficult Professor – This is not a common combination; however, you will come across this type of class at some point during your college years. This combination happens when the professor is very difficult and decides to make an easy course difficult. These are usually professors that have unrealistic or unclear expectations. In my personal experience, these are usually professors that consider teaching as their number one priority in life. I have found that professors with an active family and social life do not normally fit into this category. (It is important to note that this is only my opinion. No government studies have been completed to prove this statement.)

Researching professors and upperclassmen can help you avoid these classes. If you run across this class combination, do not become frustrated with the professor, but continue to work hard in class. It is important that you keep close track of your grades in this class by monitoring each question that was marked incorrect and following up with the professor to get the correct answer. You must be on top of each and every assignment, project, quiz, and test. Forming a good relationship with the professor is a must in this situation.

Difficult Class: Easy Professor – This combination is not a bad situation. This usually means that with an easy professor, a difficult class like statistics, for me, could be made better. No matter how hard the class is, there's a bright light when there's an easy professor. If you're struggling in the class, schedule a meeting with the professor and explain what you're finding difficult. This professor will usually spend time to help you understand. If not, at least you have made your struggles known. These professors will usually take this into consideration when deciding your grade.

In order to gain understanding, ask as many questions as needed in this class. If you are still struggling after meeting with the professor and asking questions, ask if you can do extra credit. When you have an easy professor, the opportunities are usually there to improve your grade. You must be willing to try. Take the time and make the effort!

Difficult Class: Difficult Professor – As you could guess, this is the worst combination. It requires that you never miss a class. Be on time and sit in the front of the class. Make your presence known to this professor. Pay attention and do your best. Study often for this class and do not procrastinate on group projects and other assignments. It's better to finish assignments early to give yourself time to ask the professor questions about the assignment. This situation can be frustrating, but if you try your best and build a relationship with the professor, you will make it through this class! No matter how cold or uninterested the professor seems, take the time after class to talk about the lesson or even just a quick personal chat. The professor will feel that you are interested in the course, which could help when pleading for a better grade.

There is one other challenge that many college students face with professors and that is foreign accents. Students have the privilege of being taught by qualified professors from all over the world at most colleges; however, understanding these professors can sometimes affect how we view the class. There are many students that become very frustrated and aggravated because of this issue, but it is easy to resolve.

First, I would like for you to take out a piece of paper. Write your name with whatever hand is comfortable for you, right or left. Now, write your name with the hand that you do not use often. Why was your writing not so good with the hand that is not used often? How would it feel to be judged based on the second name that you wrote? This is the same issue for professors that speak English as a second language. It's amazing that they have the courage to take a job speaking English to a room full of opinionated students. What am I saying? Be understanding! If you are taking a course from a professor that speaks English as a second language, you may need to work much harder in this class. Be on time, sit in the front of the class, read the chapter before class and if you don't understand, ask, in a polite manner, the professor to slow down. If none of these suggestions work, meet with the professor after class to review the lecture for the day. With extra effort on your part, this could be an easy class for you.

Regardless of the difficulties you face with your classes, it is important to remember that there is always help available. Most schools offer free tutoring that is included in your tuition. Check with your advisor or check your school's website for tutoring information. Also, remember that your professor is a great resource. If you're having problems grasping the information being taught, be sure that you are specific and explain the issues you are having with your professor. Also, if you are overwhelmed with work and have missed a deadline, ask for an extension. They may be willing to teach you one-on-one during their office hours. Always ask for what you need. Remember that the answer is always no if you don't ask, but if you ask there is a fifty percent chance the answer will be yes.

CHAPTER 5

Chapter 5

Grade Point Average
Study Habits and Class Attendance

The 1st semester of my freshman year was a big party! I remember thinking that I could use my same high school study methods for college and everything would work out. I would do things like write papers the night before it was due or make up lame excuses as to why my paper would be turned in late. After receiving several papers drenched in red marks, I made a few attempts to improve my grade but not enough to really help. The truth is that I took this same casual approach for most of my classes, and it all ended in the worst GPA I had received in my entire life. After a quick feeling of regret, I figured I would get it right next semester so instead of crying over spilled milk, I smiled about all of the fun I had had that semester. That ridiculous smile didn't last long. It quickly disappeared when I received a letter stating I had lost my scholarship. Suddenly, I realized I was in school, but worse, I realized my parents were going to kill me!

As a college student, good study habits are crucial to your success. Great study habits equal great grades. Bad study habits usually equal bad grades. It's that simple. There may be times when you feel you are studying hard, but your grades do not reflect your effort. If you feel this is your situation, be real with yourself. Are you actually giving your best effort? If the answer is yes, the problem could be that you need more effective study methods. Here are several tips for studying that will help improve your grades:

1. **Do not procrastinate!!** Be sure that you are aware of all tests, projects, and assignment deadlines. Use a calendar to keep

track of important dates. Once you have the dates, estimate the time it will take you to finish the task. Schedule to have the task completed about a week in advance. Some students prefer to cram for tests instead of actually learning the material. Cramming only helps you memorize the material. It will not help you if your memory fails you. Without actually learning the information, it's hard to work to your full potential and make the grades that reflect your true intelligence.

2. **Take good notes in class.** Often we miscalculate the accuracy of our memory. You think you will remember what the professor said, but later you can't recall a single word. If you write down what is being taught, it will be easy to reference later. Notes for each class should begin with the date. Put a reminder at the bottom of most important pages that states, "OVERVIEW." This section should summarize the most valuable points the professors made.

3. **Review your notes daily.** Take about an hour everyday to review your notes from each class. The hour can be broken into two 30-minute segments. This will make studying for tests much easier. Taking just ten minutes after every class to go over what you learned in class is another great strategy for making it easier to study for tests.

4. **Read and formulate questions.** Take the time to read chapters, notes, and reference materials provided in class thoroughly. Reading the material before class will allow you to follow along with the professor much easier. When reading, formulate questions to test your understanding of the material. Be sure to write down important points that may be on a test. It may be necessary to re-read chapters as you formulate questions. These questions and answers will become a convenient study guide. The study guide you create should be used as a supplement, even if you are provided a study guide by your professor.

Learning Methods

Everyone has a study method that is most effective for him or her. It could be that you learn audibly, visually, or both. If you learn best by hearing, it would be a good idea to record the professor during class or record yourself reviewing questions and answers after reading the material. If you learn best visually, you may need to rewrite the material over and over. Maybe you learn best by going to the local coffee shop, listening to music, or studying with a group of other students. If you study best in groups, join a study group or initiate one. These groups can be a great way to learn. There may be times that you miss important points from the class that another student in the group could share with you. If you decide to be a part of a study group, be sure that the students are serious. Choose students who ask questions and strive to make the best grades in class. It is important that the group is focused on studying and not socializing.

Study Scheduling

8:00 a.m.- 9:00 a.m.	Breakfast
9:00 a.m.-12:00 p.m.	Classes
12:00 p.m.- 1:00 p.m.	Lunch and study for psychology test
1:00 p.m.-3:00 p.m.	Classes
3:00 p.m.- 4:00 p.m.	Break
4:00 p.m.- 6:00 p.m.	Study for psychology test
6:00 p.m.-7:00 p.m.	Break and dinner
7:00 p.m.-9:00 p.m.	Work on English paper
9:00p.m.- 10:00 pm.	Review notes from classes

Studying can sometimes seem impossible when you have several different assignments due at one time. Even with proper study habits, this situation could become very challenging. When you are feeling overwhelmed by schoolwork, immediately create a detailed study schedule. Scheduling is the key to managing this situation. If you have a test and paper due during the same week, you should set a productive schedule every day. See the following example:

In addition to study times, schedule certain time slots throughout the day for a break. Cramming all day or night will only stress you out.

Stress prevents you from giving your best efforts. Creating a detailed schedule helps make your tasks seem less overwhelming. Stick to your plan and whatever you do, don't get frustrated and give up. Think positive, take a few deep breaths, and say, "I can do this." There is power in words and positive thinking.

Class Attendance

In addition to developing good study habits, finding your best study methods, and creating a productive schedule for studying, it is also important to attend class in order to obtain an excellent grade point average. Grade point average and class attendance go hand-in-hand. If you want a high GPA, go to class every day! Without attending class and taking great notes, you cannot keep up with what is covered in class. Some professors have strict attendance policies. A few of my professors dropped your final grade a letter for every three unexcused absences. Besides affecting your grade point average, class attendance could also provide negotiating power at the end of the semester if you need help. I learned this lesson first hand. The second semester of my freshman year, I made a D in a class that required at least a C to move on to the next course. My response to this tragedy was to do what had worked most of my life. I begged the professor to give me a C. Can you believe I was actually begging for a C—with tears and all? He listened, but then he pulled out the attendance log and told me that I had missed over six classes. My heart dropped as he could not help me because I did not try to help myself. If I had been at every class, he would have seen that I was trying. However, I was too busy sleeping in when it rained, staying in my bed when I had a headache, tooth ache, etc. As a result, I had to repeat this class in summer school. I wasted time and money by falling into the horrible habit of not attending class regularly. Regrettably, I realized this lesson too late, but now you can learn from my mistakes. Only miss classes when it is absolutely necessary.

Why should you work hard to maintain a high GPA?

Some of you may wonder, "why does is matter if my GPA is high as long as I pass?" I thought the same thing as a student because I was always told that companies mostly looked to employ students with leadership skills, ambition, and team player abilities. Less emphasis was placed on a high grade point average. The truth is that companies do look for these qualities; however, the best companies will place their hiring decisions heavily on your grade point average alone. I personally have not had any job inquire about my involvement in college activities, but I have; however, had several companies inquire about my grade point average and several of them have even required a minimum 3.0 grade point average. The following are several reasons why it is important to maintain a high grade point average:

1. **Grad schools require minimum undergraduate grade point averages.**
   When you graduate, you may decide to return to school on the graduate level. One huge requirement is a transcript from your undergraduate university. If your grade point average is below average, the admissions office of the potential university would question how you plan to be successful in graduate school if you were not successful as an undergraduate.

2. **Most executive trainee programs have a minimum grade point average requirement.**
   Executive trainee programs are college recruitment programs offered by companies that could be described as a post graduation "paid-internship". Companies use these programs to train college graduates, but they also use them to hire the best candidates from the pool of students accepted into the executive trainee program. Different companies have different requirements, but most of them attempt to recruit the best and brightest college graduates. This could be translated as students with the highest grade point averages. These programs give the company a chance to "test drive" recent college graduates before making a firm job offer.

3. **The best companies recruit the brightest and highest grade point average.**
   Most employers will use your grade point average as a measure

for determining your intelligence. The best companies which can be defined as, but not limited to, companies on the Fortune 500[4] list or companies that have a great reputation in your industry, will aggressively recruit candidates with high grade point averages. The better your GPA, the better your chances are of gaining employment with the BEST companies. These companies usually pay the best salaries.

4. **Most scholarships and financial assistance require a minimum grade point average.**
In order to maintain financial aid and scholarships, it is often required that you maintain a minimum grade point average. If money is being given or loaned to you for college tuition, it is only fair that the lender expects you to be successful in school.

Hopefully, you will gain a great education from college, but most importantly, you want a great job after college. Some people may not agree with that statement, but the bottom line is that most of us attend college to get a great job and live the good life. There is no point in attending college for two to five years and paying good money for an education if you do not put your best foot forward in obtaining your best grade point average. Many college students "do just enough to get by" without realizing that in today's society being "ok" or "average" is not enough to compete in the workforce. The effort you put into studying will reflect in your grades, which may ultimately decide the type of companies that will be attracted to you. So, do your best.

---

4 Fortune 500 – This is a list compiled by Fortune magazine of the top publicly owned (traded on the stock market) companies in the USA. The companies are qualified by their profits or gross revenues.

CHAPTER 6

Chapter 6

Overcoming Obstacles

At some point during your college years you will face obstacles. Your obstacles can be a minor as a difficult roommate or as major as the death of a loved one. Your biggest challenge is to finish college with a degree no matter how big the obstacle. The following are personal stories of college students or graduates that have faced and overcome major obstacles. From their stories I hope that you gain hope and strength to overcome whatever obstacles may come your way.

Dana's Story – Difficult Professors Lead to Successful Endings

When I was a college sophomore, I had let go of the "done in four years" dream. I had just chosen graphic design as my field of study not knowing that deciding so late would delay my graduation date. As time passed, I felt that I didn't fit in with the program structure. It seemed that no matter what I did my class projects were never good enough. My teachers would tell me that I was doing a good job on a project and then give me a C+ (and in art school, a C is like a D). Once, I remember getting an A on an assignment. It was hanging up in the hallway and I was so proud. Then, the next day, I noticed that my professor knocked the grade down to a B+. Things like this were constantly happening to me and it began to affect my confidence and my self-esteem. I eventually quit trying to win my teachers' respect and I started ditching class. I stayed in my dorm room for days at a time. I was really discouraged and I had no confidence in myself at all. Bouts of depression overwhelmed me constantly and even one of my professors suggested that I seek psychological counseling. (He didn't know he was part of my problem). My grades steadily slipped until I was kicked out of the art program and lost my scholarship my junior year. At the time, this seemed to be the lowest point in my life.

At that point, with such a low GPA, the idea of graduating seemed unattainable. I became jealous of anyone who got out of school on time and landed a good job. My confidence was shaken so much that I was afraid to apply for a job at a local McDonalds for fear of sucking **at that as well. I considered** leaving school and not majoring in art at all, until my parents suggested that I transfer to the university in my hometown and study graphic design there. I went to this school's art department website and I was so impressed. I saw student work that was full of originality. I knew that was what I needed—an art program that would allow me the room to develop my own style. I transferred to this school my fourth year of college and immediately saw improvement in my grades. I took some classes over again—even though I had gained transfer credits—because I wanted to show the faculty at my new school that I was serious about getting acclimated to their program structure. It all paid off. I've won design competitions and have had my work in local publications.

During my fifth year of college or "2nd" senior year, I became pregnant and had to sit out a semester. It was difficult, but I used that time to my advantage and began working as a graphic design freelancer. I let those projects substitute for the classes I would have taken. Because of the freelance, my design and conceptual skills were stronger than ever when I returned to school. I graduated my sixth year of college, full of knowledge and experience. Two months after graduation, I landed a really great design internship at a prestigious direct marketing firm. I continue freelancing because I have built up a steady stream of clients. I look forward to establishing my own design agency in the future.

Derrick's Story – College Is Truly for Everyone

I would never forget it! The results of my ACT score came back. I vividly remembered my teachers informing me to eat a good wholesome breakfast as well as instructing me to be well rested for the big test day. I failed to follow their advice on both fronts. As a result, little effort was put forth in making a passing score. It is called self-sabotage. In my mind, I had no plans of going to college, at least that's what I thought. Anyway, I was deeply curious about what the college experience would be like and what it could offer me. Simply put, the real problem was fear. I feared rejection. I feared accepting a challenge. I feared failure, and most of all, I feared myself. I feared being smart and intelligent in my anti-education environment. I was extremely afraid and intimidated of becoming a college student. I felt, at the time, that I was unprepared for higher learning. Here was the equation in my mind: Disadvantaged school + disadvantaged community + an average student who lacked confidence = failure. With that said, my poor performing ACT score confirmed that reality. The score I received was embarrassing to mention—even today. It was a shameful 13. Despite my emotional state of mind, test score, and social barriers, somewhere in the depths of my soul, I managed to overcome my marred identity convincing myself that receiving a college education was my destiny. How did I go about pursuing a college education? I didn't have the ACT score. I didn't have the money. And I only had average grades. I discovered that one only needs courage to confront their deepest fears. Ironically, I did something that I thought I would never do. I joined the military, namely, the United States Navy.

It was official! I had signed on the dotted lines to be an enlisted member of the United States Navy. I had made a gigantic decision to serve my country even though I needed my mother's consent due to my age. In return I could learn a trade, earn a living, travel the world, and participate in the college-funding program -- that is the Montgomery G.I. Bill. What a terrific tradeoff I thought! Here I was, seventeen years old, at the airport for the very first time, waiting to arrive to my first duty station along with four other Navy recruits. Filled with the dual sentiments of nervousness and excitement, and entering into the unknown, I wondered what this new life would be like. In the midst of all of the uncertainties and unanswered questions within myself, there were two things that gave me assurance. The assurances were that the military would provide a great "opportunity" and that the military would provide a great "experience" for me.

When I look back on my military career, the good far outweighed the bad. Even though I was dissatisfied with most of my job assignments, it indeed afforded me the opportunity to earn a decent living, travel the world, and participate in the G.I. Bill. I guess three out of four isn't bad. Because of my dissatisfying job assignments, sweeping, swabbing decks, and cleaning toilets, attending college was constantly on my radar. It became a necessity because it was the driving force of why I joined the military. In my final year in the Navy, I was able to advance out of menial duties. This advancement would have given me an opportunity to earn a nice hefty pay raise, but I decided not to re-enlist. I wanted to pursue my childhood dream of becoming self-employed. In order to realize the dream of becoming a business owner, higher learning was the answer and my next big move, especially with money not being a critical issue.

Living an hour outside of Seattle, Washington at the time, I pondered what would be my next destination. I had become attached to Seattle in some ways, mainly because of the scenery of the evergreen trees, the great jobs, the nightlife, the diversity, and the friendships I created with my fellow shipmates. However, it rained entirely too often and I missed the South more than I wanted to admit. Instead of going back home to Memphis, Tennessee, I considered Columbus, Georgia because my cousin was stationed there and we were very cool. It was there where the road of higher learning began.

As you would imagine, I had been away from school for a while—three years. One of the first things I had to do was to take a college aptitude examination. As you probably predicted, I did not do too well. Before taking "real college courses", enrollment in developmental courses in subjects such as English and Mathematics was required. And I totally agreed; I needed the refreshment. The purpose of the developmental courses was to refresh my memory and enhance my skill sets as it relates to the fundamentals of higher learning. I performed at a high level and appreciated every lesson in every class. I was driven. I was focused and had a more mature outlook towards education. I was determined not to take this learning opportunity for granted like I did in high school. What really motivated me was the fact that there was a time when people of African descent in this country suffered, struggled, and even died for people like me to enjoy the simple freedoms of reading, writing, etc. So, with that said, I was determined that their sufferings and sacrifices would not be in vain. With the personal and historical motivations, I became a member of the Student Government Association (SGA) and Honors Academy. I was nominated for Who's Who in American Colleges, won several competitive scholarships, and I graduated with honors on the two-year and four-year college level.

Deondra's Story – When Your Roommate Doesn't Work Out

Being away from home isn't the easiest thing in the world, but having a bad roommate makes it even worse. When I came to college I decided to be open minded to different things and different people. Having an open mind didn't mean doing things and hanging with people who were outside of my character.

The first time I was away from my family, I had to move in with someone who had lived and been raised completely different from me. My roommate was gross! She left food out for days, dirty clothes out for weeks, and she didn't wash her hands after she used the bathroom. She had been sheltered for her entire life, so when she moved out on her on she went wild. I will never forget the night she had guys over. She lied about her age and did everything in her power to keep her friends from talking to me, but it didn't work. I became so frustrated. I just wanted to go home. I prayed that God would fix the situation. I talked to her about the problems that I had with her the very best way that I knew how; however, it seemed like nothing worked. It only got worse. Everybody who knows me knows that I love to talk. There were days that we would sit in the very same dorm room and not say one word to each other. One of her family members who is much older than both of us was over everyday. She had the worse attitude in the world. I talked to my family and friends about the entire situation. I received a mixture of advice. Some suggested that I pray about the situation, while others offered some not so nice advice. Praying was the last thing that I wanted to do. Telling her what was on my mind was looking more like it, but I did the right thing, I prayed and talked to my RA (Resident Advisor).

We (my roommate, the RA, and I) had a meeting. By the end of the meeting it was decided that she would move out. After she moved out I didn't have a roommate for about two and a half months. Looking at my other friends, I realized I was missing out on having a good roommate. The news about the vacancy was out and potential roommates were coming to meet me and take a look at the room. It was great because -- in a way -- I was able to choose my own roommate. In the end I got the best roommate that I could have ever asked for. It's still not easy being away from home, but I'm doing a lot better. I made a 3.425 GPA my first semester of college. The experience with my first roommate has made me truly appreciate my current roomie.

Selwyn's Story – Finishing School After Experiencing a Tragedy

It was Friday April 10th, the spring semester of my freshman year. It was a couple of weeks before finals and everyone was dreading that horrible time of the year. Then late that evening I received a phone call from my brother with the worst news imaginable. He had taken our father to the hospital because he was extremely ill. He was only given a few hours to live, 24 at the most. I was in complete shock by this startling phone call. I immediately attempted to get a flight home as soon as possible. I arrived home Saturday morning only to find my father in a coma, unresponsive to any of our tears or pleading for him to wake up. The hardest part was to see my father, the strongest, greatest man I knew reduced to a mere mortal filled with tubes and hooked to life support. Seemingly, as if on cue, after my last brother had arrived in town on Sunday April 10th, my father passed away. This was by far the hardest experience of my college career, in fact, the hardest experience of my life. With the pain and heartbreak I was feeling at this time, I honestly wanted nothing to do with school. But I remember how vocal my father was about me completing my education, just as my other 6 brothers and my sister had done. I withdrew from all of my classes the semester of my father's death and accepted a grade of incomplete. The following semester, I took a full load of classes and also worked to complete all missed work to remove the grade of incomplete. Currently, all work has been completed and I am on track for graduation in May 2009. The pain of losing a father is something I hope no one has to experience. Every time I come home it is difficult because it is strange not seeing his bright smiling face, but I rest in the fact that he is no longer in pain and now is in eternal peace. With the support of friends and family I have been able to overcome this tragedy. I forever uphold his legacy and try to live by the values he instilled in me while trying my hardest to make him proud.

CHAPTER 7

Chapter 7

IS YOUR MAJOR RIGHT FOR YOU?

After your high school graduation, the pressure is on. Everyone knows that you are on your way to college and the big questions being thrown at you from every direction are: "What are you going to college for?", "What are you going to major in?", and "What do you want to be?" Some people will go as far as suggesting a profession and major for you based on their expertise, how much money you could make, or the connections they already have in a field that is familiar to them. Unfortunately, these questions will continue to be thrown at you throughout your four to five years of college from any and everyone that finds out that you are in college. Some students feel so pressured to answer these questions that they decide on a major haphazardly just to appease the persistent inquisitive friends or family members who will not let them rest until an answer is given that satisfies them. The expectation for you to know what you want to be and do after graduation can be a lot of pressure. Most freshmen begin with only a vague idea of what they want to do after college. This is okay. How can you know what career you want to work in 4 to 5 years from now? It can be difficult, but this chapter will provide you with a guide on how to decide a major.

In order to answer the question that this title asks, you first need to evaluate the following:

Step 1 - What are your passions and strengths?
Step 2 - What careers are available that fit your passion and strengths?
Step 3 - What major will best prepare you for these careers?

What are your passions and strengths?

To answer this question, grab a pen and paper. Write a list of your favorite classes over the years, the classes that you excelled in, and what you enjoy most in general. Take as much time as you need and make the list as long as possible. It is important for you to understand that choosing a career that you enjoy may mean choosing a life that you enjoy. The culture at many companies is a 9 to 11 hour workday. Since jobs require so many hours, it is important that this time is spent working a job that you enjoy. You will only be your best when you are working in a career that you love. The next step in determining your passion and interest is to take an interest inventory test. Tests such as the Strong Interest Inventory® test ask several questions to determine your interests, strengths, and weaknesses. The results of the test will marry your interests with several career options. Most college career centers offer these tests. This assessment is not required for anyone. However, I suggest taking it even if you've chosen a major. Your results may open your eyes to new possibilities. I visited the career advisement center, took an interest assessment test, and was pointed in the right direction. I originally was a pre-med major. After taking a few course related to this major, I quickly realized that if I had to take another three semesters of similar courses, I would not make it. I changed my major to fashion merchandising. It was one of the best decisions I've made in my life.

What careers are available that fit your passion?

Once you have completed step one, the next step is to make a list of all the careers that you know would fit your passion, interests, and strengths. How do you find these careers? The results from your interest test assessment, career fairs, and the Internet will be very helpful. The results from your interest test will not only open your eyes to interests and strengths that you possess, but it will also provide you with a suggested list of careers that may be the right fit for you.

Career fairs also offer great information about different careers. These fairs give students the opportunity to speak with employers about potential careers. If possible, you should attend every career fair that comes to your university and other universities in the area. While speaking with different companies, you may be surprised to hear of a job you didn't know existed. This is your time to interview the person that may potentially hire you one day. When approaching a representative at a career fair, it is important to be very professional. Have a list of questions typed and prepared before you enter a career fair. The questions should include information on the different positions available in the company, what employers like most about the company, and also questions about the majors that they employ. This is a great time to ask an employer about positions available in their company that would fit your passion. Visit as many booths as possible and have a resume to distribute to potential employers. Go to chapter 11 for information on creating a resume. If you speak with representatives that have jobs interesting to you, ask if you can come into the office for an informational interview about the position. Be sure to ask for a business card and follow up by email. If you're still interested after the informational interview, ask if they would allow you to shadow a person in that position for a week. Career fairs are sometimes taken for granted by students. These are excellent opportunities for students at all levels, from freshmen to seniors.

In addition to career fairs, the Internet is another great way to research different career options. There are several websites that offer advice on choosing a career based on your passion, interests, and strengths. You could also just type in a phrase such as "choosing a career", "careers in math", or "careers in art".

Once you have found a few careers that interest you, research all of the details concerning these careers such as the starting salary and job requirements. After you have this information, begin the process of gaining experience in these areas by securing internships, informational interviews, or shadowing someone that works in that field.

What major will best prepare you for these careers?

Now that you have a found a few career options, you should decide what majors will best prepare you for these careers. Most students decide a major and then try to find what careers are available in that major, but that is not the correct way to choose a major. When you are deciding on a restaurant for dinner, normally the process is to figure out what type of food you want to eat and then find a restaurant that has that type of food. The same is true when deciding a major. Find the careers that interest you and then find the majors that will best prepare you for that career. The best way to find this information is to call a company that has this job available. Introduce yourself to the human resources manager, tell that person the job you're interested in, and ask what majors they suggest that will best prepare you for that career. Because you shouldn't depend on one resource, call and ask several companies the same question. Also, look on the Internet for this job on a web-based career site and check to see if they require any particular major. Based on the information you've received from actual companies and a few web-based job banks, decide your major.

By now you should have a major in mind, potential job interests, job requirements, and the salary range. The last step is to start a list of companies that offer the job you're interested in. Search for details such as hours, company culture, and dress code. The idea is to research and interview companies that will work for you. Start planning early. If the companies you research will require you to wear suits everyday, begin to purchase suits during your college years. It's never too early to prepare for what's to come after graduation. Also, you can start preparing yourself by reaching out to recruitment managers for summer internship programs or executive trainee programs. Executive trainee programs are similar to internships but are offered after graduation. Many companies offer executive trainee programs. These programs allow you to experience a company hands on as well as allow the company to see if you're a candidate they would want to hire. Be sure to look for these programs and locate the name of the recruiter or human resource person that is over that program. We will explore this subject in more detail in the next chapter.

Summary and Additional Points to Remember When Deciding on a Major:

- ✓ Do not be afraid to choose a career path that is less traveled. You will only work to your full potential when you are working in a career you love.
- ✓ Do not base your career decision on how much money you think you will make. The amount of money you make is up to you.
- ✓ Know the requirements for the career or job you're interested in. Some jobs require post-graduate work such as a master's degree or doctorate degree. It may even be necessary that you have experience in an entry-level position. In order to gain experience, you may have to complete an internship. Whatever the job requirements, be sure that you know them when you choose your major.
- ✓ Know the starting salary for your career field of interest. One big shock to many college graduates is their starting salary. Be prepared by knowing the salary range for an entry-level position in your field of study. Also, research the salary for an experienced employee. In order to find salary information, ask someone who works in the field. Check websites such as salary.com or other sites that provide salary information. Do not be discouraged if your starting salary is low. Money will come with time, experience, and your performance.

Changing Your Major

If you decide, for some reason, that you want to change your major, check possibilities before making this decision. If you feel your career goal has changed, research at least three companies in that field to determine if the change is necessary. You can usually call any human resource office. Tell them your situation quickly and ask if you can still be employed for that job with your current major. For example, if you decide to be an attorney and your major is currently communications, you may not need to change to pre-law. Research the requirements and determine if you can get into law school with a communications degree. As a matter of fact, you will find that law school admissions are determined more by your score on the LSAT test than your undergraduate major. So, instead of wasting your time changing your major, channel that energy into studying for the LSAT. Also, you have the option to add a major and become a double major in college. You can even add an additional field of study to minor in. Changing or adding a major may lengthen your time in school, but if it's absolutely necessary, it's well worth it.

The Proof is in the Punchline

Witness #4: Justin Bird

Who is your current employer?
- Mt. Sinai School of Medicine

What is your occupation?
- Chief Resident – Orthopedic Surgery
- Author, The Menses File (themensesfile.com) – I took a couple of English courses in college, creative writing, etc. The summer after I finished college I started writing. Initially, I was interested in writing movies, so I found a few scripts online and used them as templates to develop my own script. I wrote a couple scripts, and then after I read a James Patterson book that my cousin left with me, I decided that I could put another story idea I had into book form.

What was your major in college?
- Undergrad – Africana Studies (Cornell University).
- Mt. Sinai School of Medicine.

Why did you choose this major?
- Undergrad – I was interested in it. I started out as biology major, but the introductory courses weren't interesting. I sat down with my advisor and she encouraged me to look through the syllabus and find something that I would be interested in.
- Medicine – My mom is a nurse and went to nursing school when I was 12. I found it rewarding to see her studying for nursing school and taking care of people. In college I played sports, both wrestling and football. During that time, I was exposed to our team physician, an orthopedic surgeon. I spent time in his office and was impressed with how he took care of us and his patients. He sparked my interest in orthopedic surgery. My mom also knew some orthopedic surgeons who worked in the same hospital as she did. I went to their office and saw their patients with them. I saw what they did on a day-to-day basis and even had the great benefit of seeing surgeries performed. During one my undergrad summers, I volunteered in the ER.
- Program – Minority Medical Education Program (A Federally Funded Program). During one of my undergraduate summers, I had the amazing experience of working with this program in Chicago. I was with a group of students who wanted to do the same things I did. This program helped prepare us for the required exams to get into medical school.

How did you get your current job? Explain your career path.
- Summer Programs
- Internships

What was your first job out of college?
- Columbia University – I had to finish one more course, but I also needed a job. I tried to find a job in a lab but ended up taking a job taking care

of animals that were used in research. It was a dirty job, but well worth it because there were professional people in that setting who wrote recommendations for me to get in medical school. One of the veterinarians there became my mentor. Ten years later, he is still my mentor.

How did you get this job?

- I would go to Columbia University and check their job postings. I did this every week. I finally got a call back.

What advice would you give a college student concerning finding a job after college, how to choose a major, or any subject related?

- Look for something you're passionate about, something you feel is worthwhile.

Witness #5: Leslie Waller

Who is your current employer?

- A Fortune 500 Food Company

What is your title?

- Sr. Associate Brand Manager

What was your major in college?

- The program I chose was a five-year Master's of Business Administration program (3 year undergraduate/2 years graduate)
- Concentration: Marketing. As I was rather certain about what I wanted to do, I locked into this type of program.

Why did you choose this major?

- I felt it would utilize a lot of my strengths. While I was in high school, I participated in various extracurricular activities such as Majorette, Band, Choir, Show Choir, Student Council, Volleyball, and Basketball. I held several leadership roles in these activities.

How did you get your current job? Explain your career path.

- When I finished college, my first job was more sales driven. I eventually was promoted to a marketing focused position, but I didn't feel that I was getting the experience that I needed for my development. After five years, I decided to look for other opportunities. I attended the National Black MBA Association Conference Career Fair and interviewed for a position with my current employer. I was extended an invitation to interview on site. After the interview, I went back to the airport and before I could board the plane, they called and offered me the position!

What was your first job out of college? How did you get this job?

- My first position out of college was with Ford Motor Company as a zone manager. I interned with Ford the summer prior to accepting a permanent offer.

What advice would you give a college student concerning finding a job after college, how to choose a major, or any subject related?

- Use your resources. Don't overuse all of the technology that's out there to determine your area of interest. There is nothing like real life experiences. Seek out those people who have traveled the road you'd like to travel and use their experiences as your teachers. Volunteer in your guidance department at school or in the career center at your college. Use this information to find out what's the best college or the best company to gain the experience you'll need to be marketable and ultimately successful.

A Special Note to You

I can still remember my junior year of college. My best friend and I were still awake at 3:00 a.m. talking about how terrified we were of graduating. After all the hard work, papers, tests, and money spent, here we were, afraid to graduate. This may sound crazy to people that didn't go to college or even crazier to parents, but for other undergraduates this probably sounds very familiar. How many times do you even think about the fact that the real purpose of college is to get a good paying job, while becoming an independent, responsible adult? It's funny that, while in school, you're so busy being a student that you don't have time to recognize the purpose of being a student.

Now it is time for some of the best advice you'll ever receive. First things first, get a pen and paper. Now write down why you are going to college. Be totally honest with yourself. Regardless of what you wrote, the main reason you are going to college is to get a good job. All you've ever been told is that without an education, it's hard to find a good job. That's what the whole universe is preaching, but let me put something else in your head. An education and no preparation will make it almost impossible to find a good job right out of college. If you don't believe me, find 10 people you know that have been to college and ask them what happened right after they graduated. Probably six out of those 10 people are not doing what they went to school for. Several of them probably don't even need the degree they have to perform their current job. If you don't want this to be you, PLEASE LISTEN TO ME!!! I am going to give you five points that will almost guarantee you the job you want when you graduate.

1. *Meet contacts while in college.*
2. *Keep your GRADE POINT AVERAGE at a 3.5 or better.*
3. *Complete at least three internships successfully.*
4. *Make the most out of every opportunity.*
5. *Keep a positive attitude.*

READY FOR THE REAL WORLD?

CHAPTER 8

Chapter 8

The Punchline

As you have already read in the introduction, my motivation for writing this book was the frustration I felt as a recent college graduate. I was unable to find the job I had dreamed about during my 4 years as an undergraduate student. The unfortunate truth is that every year there are thousands of college graduates who feel this exact same way. They walk across the stage to receive their degree, are filled with great hope of success, and look forward to a great job in their near future. This hope quickly dissipates as reality begins to creep in and the search for that perfect job begins. This is when college graduates discover that a college degree alone is not enough. With no experience, the frustration of being rejected by desired employers over and over can take a toll on anyone. This feeling causes some grads to take "any" job that pays. If you've ever wondered why your cousin with an accounting degree is working as a sales associate, or your friend with an art degree works at the bank, you now have your answer. To understand the importance of experience from an employer's perspective, consider the following scenario. This is kind of farfetched, but just go with it.

> Scenario 1: Mark decides to try out for a team. The team requires great athletic ability and $2,000 for the uniform. Because it has been Mark's dream to be a part of this team, he spends a significant amount of time working to earn the $2,000. In tryouts, the coach announces that he needs one of the candidates for a game tonight, but there is no time to have everyone actually try out. To Mark's surprise there are hundreds of candidates at the coach's office waiting for the opportunity

to play on this team and they all have the $2,000 required. His chance to speak to the coach finally arrives. He does his best to convince the coach that he is the best candidate. The coach inquires about his experience. Mark gets really nervous because he never took the time to play for any intramural teams on campus, nor does he have any references to vouch for his skills. Mark spent all of his time working to get the $2,000 that was required. Before Mark, the coach met with many other candidates that had their money, but most importantly, these candidates also had successfully played on similar teams and they had references to vouch for their skills. The coach deliberates because, after all, Mark does seem very sincere.

As a coach what would be your decision? In the real world, the decision is easy. The coach would choose the players with experience and references. The money in this scenario represents a college degree. Employers will respect your college degree and the effort you put into obtaining it; however, when another candidate has a degree, experience, and references, the decision is much easier. The candidate with experience will almost always be chosen. So, how do you gain the experience that you need to be chosen for the team? Internships, volunteer opportunities, part-time jobs relevant to your major, shadowing, and study abroad programs are all great opportunities to gain experience that employers' desire.

Internships

An internship (paid or unpaid) is one of the best methods to try out jobs within your field of interest. The goal of an internship is to gain experience, meet contacts, retain references, and hopefully, secure a job offer upon graduation. A misconception that students often have is that internships are for graduating seniors. If you wait until your senior year to complete your 1st internship, it may be too late. Internships can be completed as early as your freshman year of college. I suggest that you complete at least 3 internships before you graduate.

Volunteer

The main purpose of volunteering is to meet people within your industry. You've heard the statement, "It's not what you know, it's who you know." Well, this is very true. Connections will be crucial to your success in finding a job after graduation. We will talk more about this in the next chapter. There are opportunities all around you to volunteer, but you must take the time to search for them. Look for volunteer opportunities within your industry. For example, if you're interested in the medical field, volunteer at a local hospital for the summer. Networking can also be done through events such as: building a house for Habitat for Humanity, assisting the American Red Cross, or raising money for Avon's Walk for Breast Cancer. During any volunteer job, it is vitally important that you make your career interest known. Do not work so hard to gain a great reputation and rapport during this time without letting people know your career interest.

Part-time Jobs

When college students need extra cash, they are not usually discriminatory about the type of job they take. What do you think could happen if students actually decided to work part-time jobs related to their majors? Choose jobs that could put you in close proximity to individuals working in the area you desire to work in. A theatre major may decide to work the ticket sales counter at the local theatre instead of working as a waitress. A pre-law major may opt for working as a receptionist at a local law firm instead of working as a bartender. Being in close proximity to other individuals in your industry helps you become more knowledgeable, make connections, and adds value to your resume.

Shadowing

Shadowing is spending some time with a professional person to gain knowledge of that person's job functions and the qualities needed to perform that job. It is a great way to get hands-on knowledge of a particular job. Receiving this opportunity requires that you first make a connection with an individual in a job that seems interesting to you and then request an opportunity to shadow them for a day or maybe a week. During this time you will silently sit with this person while they are performing their job duties. You will have questions, but remember that this person is performing a job and will not have time to stop and answer all of your questions. Formulate a list of questions and then request a lunch or breakfast meeting. Review your questions with him/her during this meeting.

Study Abroad

Study abroad programs are offered at most colleges and universities. The world is becoming more global and business is following suit. Studying in foreign countries provide students with knowledge about other cultures, exposure to new ideas and people, and the opportunity to travel. Having a study abroad experience on your resume offers you an edge over other candidates. Check the websites of potential employers for foreign business affairs. Research the trend of your industry to see what countries are vital parts of that industry and look for study abroad opportunities in those countries. For example, if your major is robotics engineering, a great place to study abroad is Japan, the world's leading country in robotics. If you were to apply with an engineering firm, this study abroad experience would immediately place you at an advantage. Some countries will naturally be a good pick if you aren't sure where to study abroad. For example, in 2007, the US imports from China was worth over 321 billion dollars. With the rapid increase of imports coming from China, most companies in the US have an interest in this country. Study abroad programs can be expensive, so plan early and apply for any scholarships or grants awarded to candidates for the programs.

You must actively pursue each of these options to gain experience. These opportunities can be found through many sources including contacts made at career fairs, volunteer events, networking, or the school's career center. The lack of time should never be an excuse for not gaining experience that will be valuable to your future after graduation. Think about Mark in the scenario above. Remember that you are competing, and you want to be the candidate that walks in the door with all of the items Mark didn't have. Many companies will work around your school schedule, especially if you're volunteering or completing an unpaid internship. Having experience is not a luxury, but a requirement, if you want your post graduation process to go smoothly.

The Proof is in the Punchline

Witness #6: Erik Pettie

Who is your current employer?
- A major record label

What is your title?
- Senior Director of Digital Marketing and Strategy

What was your major in college?
- Marketing – Undergrad – University of Maryland, College Park
- Master's – Music and Entertainment Professions - NYU

Why did you choose this major?
- Marketing – I was initially looking to major in Advertising. However, that wasn't the most common major among schools at the time. Once accepted to UM, marketing was the closest option.
- Master's – Music and Entertainment Professions – I knew I would be motivated to finish a Master's in this field. I wasn't interested in any another course of study. I knew it would be difficult to be in a new city like New York trying to work and pay bills. Moving to New York to pursue a master's degree was a strategic move. Being a student offered me living security since my housing was funded by loans. Therefore, I was able to focus on additional internships and part-time work in my field. Because I went straight into grad school from undergrad, I was basically able to extend my student experience a few years to obtain more contacts and relevant work experience.

How did you get your current job? Explain your career path.
- I went the road most traveled via internships and volunteer work within my major. My first internship was with an independent record store chain then I went on to a major music distributor. I also worked at the campus radio and TV stations while at UMCP. My current job was referred to me by a friend who was also an industry advisor. I actually didn't have a lot of experience for this job, but I got very high recommendations from my pervious jobs and had extensive experience marketing music. The way the business is changing, I have been able to grow with the position to maximize my efforts.

What advice would you give a college student concerning finding a job after college, how to choose a major, or any subject related?
- Follow your interests in terms of picking a major and a school. Start early to find a job. Intern and meet new people. Utilize your electives and take

some things that are not in your major that may tickle your interest. It will all come together in the end. A lot of people party for three years and then try to cram everything into their last year. It doesn't work well that way!

What general life advice would you give a college student?
- Learn balance. You can have fun and still get your work done. Develop a level of tunnel vision and know when to use it. You need to know what's going on around you, but don't let it govern your steps. Some people are in school and land a job their sophomore year. That doesn't work for everyone. You must work your own plan and it will work out for you in the end.

Last Words – When I was sitting in class in the 11th grade, I had no idea how my life would turn out. I have been able to get where I am basically through trial and error. That's the only way to really figure out what works for you.

Witness #7: Clarence Nesbitt

Who is your current employer?
- A global sports apparel company

What is your title?
- Assistant General Counsel – My specialty is corporate and general business law.

What was your major in college?
> College – Florida Agricultural & Mechanical University (FAMU)
>> o Undergraduate Major: Business Administration
>> o Master's: Business Administration
- Law School – Georgetown University Law Center

Why did you choose this major?
- Business – It was the most practical to me. It allowed me to find a job after four years and didn't require a graduate degree.
- Law School – As I wasn't satisfied with my career options after completing my MBA, I thought this professional degree would give me additional flexibility and open more doors.

How did you get your current job? Explain your career path.
- I went to law school and then found a summer associate position at Shearman and Sterling, LLP. in New York as a second-year law student. This led to a full-time job as an associate after I graduated from Georgetown. I worked at Shearman for 3 ½ years. Thereafter, I started working with my current

employer, a global sports apparel company. I decided to leave my previous employer because I wanted to come to a company where I saw potential for a long-term career and that also was in an industry that excited me.

How did you get your first job out of college?

- Since I went to law school immediately after college, my first full-time job was at Shearman and Sterling and that was obtained through the law school's career placement office.

CHAPTER 9

Chapter 9

NETWORKING CREATING AND UTILIZING YOUR RESOURCES

As a college student you may equate the word "networking" to "sucking up". This is exactly how I felt as a student, and because I was determined to always "keep it real", I dismissed any form of networking that made me uncomfortable. During a recent walk through Central Park with a friend, I listened as she also shared her disgust with that word. As a college student she equated networking with being phony. She suggested replacing the word "networking" with "connecting". In this chapter, I will move forward with her suggestion by using the term connecting as much as possible. Networking is as simple as connecting with another individual. The 3 steps to connecting are making an introduction and a great impression, and following up. Regardless of how you feel about this subject you must understand that connecting is absolutely necessary and will be critical in the process of finding a job after college. Some students will find a job through an ad in the paper, filling out applications, or posting a resume on-line. However, the single most important method of securing a job is networking or referrals. According to experts, most jobs are found through networking. We are drawn to familiarity and the same goes for employers. The saying, "It's not what you know, it's who you know," applies heavily to finding a job or internship.

Have you seen the movie, "Pay it Forward"? The concept was that you do something good for one person and that person is obligated to do something good for 3 others, and so on. After a while, the network of good deeds was huge! When you connect with one individual, you are tapping into their network. The following is a scenario of how networking can spread. On an internship you meet Dwayne, a manager at the company. After sharing your career goals with him, he introduces you to Rosa, another associate at the company. You and Rosa meet for a lunch date and after discussing your career goals, she decides to forward your resume to her brother, the vice-president of a major corporation. Although Dwayne was not able to assist you directly with your career goals, he was able to connect you with others that could help. See the following graph for an example of connecting:

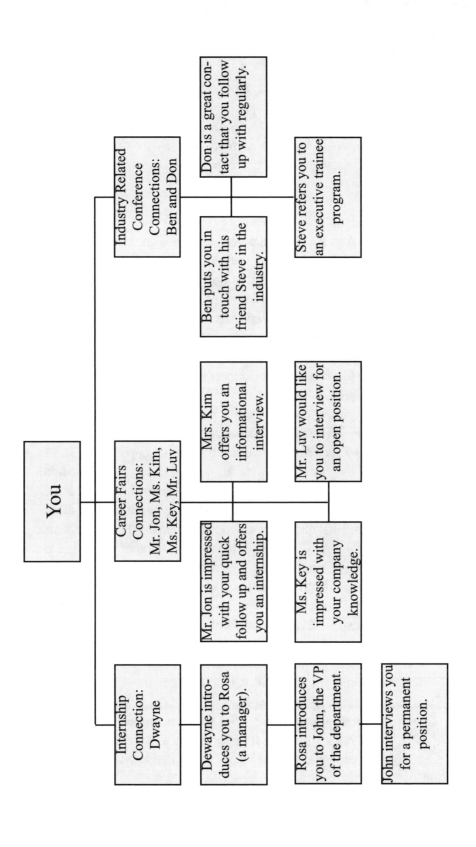

As you can see, your network can be as big as you make it. Imagine what would happen
if you began to connect with 2 people a week! If you began as a freshman, you would have many job options by the time you are a senior. There are many different opportunities to network. These include, but are not limited to, the following:

- **On the Job** – Your next opportunity may come through a co-worker. It is best that you work at a company related to your industry; however, even if you are working at a local restaurant, there is always an opportunity to connect with new people. A connection made while on the job is perfect because a co-worker or even a customer can attest to your character, work ethic, and attitude.
- **Internship** – On an internship, you have two options: 1) Get lost in the shuffle or 2) Connect with the managers and other employees in the company. The connections built during an internship could secure a permanent position with that company. The connections made on an internship may also be a great referral or reference for another opportunity. There are many ways to network during an internship. One method is to ask a manager or co-worker out to lunch. If you secure a lunch appointment, you should have intelligent questions prepared that may help provide guidance for your future. This is the time to share your career goals. Another method is to request a 10 minute meeting with a person in the company that you identify as a possible mentor. This person may have the position that you want in 5 years or they may be well respected in the company. Again, once this meeting is confirmed, have questions prepared and share your goals. It is important to always ask how they made it to their current position and make sure you follow up with a "thank you" email or hand-written note.
- **Volunteer Opportunity** – As mentioned in the last chapter, this is one of the easiest opportunities to take advantage of. Volunteer opportunities are all around you. If you are on an

internship, volunteer for special projects to connect with new people, or volunteer with a company in your industry. Another option is to find a non-profit in your area and volunteer. During volunteer assignments, share your career goals with your new contacts and keep in touch with individuals that you meet. Your new contacts may be able to connect with someone that could help you with your career goals.

- **Industry Related Conference** – Conferences related to your industry are the perfect place to network with individuals from all over the country and maybe the world. Professionals attend conferences to learn new information but also to network. It is imperative that you have a business card and request business cards from others. In order to prepare for future personal notes, write a brief note on the back of the business cards you receive that will remind you of that person. Then follow up and stay in touch.

- **At Church** – Use your contacts at church to spread the word about your career ambitions. Ask around to see if anyone works in your industry that could offer you advice on finding a job or general knowledge of his or her career path.

- **Family and Friends** – Family and friends are your best sources for networking because they are usually your personal cheerleaders. These are the people that want to see you do well more than anyone; however, they sometimes forget your career interest. So, it is important that you remind them often of your career goals. Ask your family and friends to think of two successful people that would be willing to speak with you about your career goals. It does not matter if that person works in your industry or not. Remember you never know whom they may know.

- **Career Fairs** - Employers take the time to visit college campuses to find new recruits. So, be sure that you are a recruit they would want to follow up with. Do your research on the companies that will be in attendance at the fair. Draft a few questions related to positions in the company as well as general questions about the company. Arrive at the career fair as soon as it opens so that you will meet recruiters while they are awake and fresh. Dress appropriately with a jacket or blazer, and slacks, or skirt -- if you are a woman. Look sharp. Bring a cover letter and resume specific to the companies that interest you. Many students do not take advantage of career fairs, but these fairs are the best places to meet contacts that are in a position to hire you directly. Always provide your business card to the recruiter and ask for a business card in return. Treat a career fair as you would an interview. Follow up with every contact you meet with a personal note of thanks and request an informational interview.

- **College Professors** – The professors who teach courses in your major usually have contacts in the field from previous experience. If you have made a good impression and have built a great professional relationship, your professor could help you find an internship or a job. Take the time to appear interested in class, meet with your professor, share your career goals, and ask about any possible opportunities that may be available in your major.

- **Students** – This is the resource that college students take for granted the most. Your peers will be professionals in a few years. Many graduates discover job openings from other students. The best method of meeting new students is to join organizations on campus such as the student government. Broaden your horizon and join organizations with diverse membership.

Networking can be very intimidating. Even very experienced individuals have a hard time connecting with strangers, but the more you do it the easier it becomes. In order to network, I suggest that you have self-confidence, a business card, and great follow-up.

When networking, the potential contact must feel that you are confident. You are selling yourself and if you do not believe in yourself, no one else will. When you meet a new contact, take a deep breath, and remember that they are a person just like you.

Even if you have no job title, you should have a business card. It is not likely that you have a resume on you in the grocery store; however, it is very likely that you could meet a great contact there and will need to give this person a way to contact you. I suggest having an attractive business card made with your name and contact information. Remember that your card is a representative of you, so make sure that they are professionally produced. Business cards can be made at a local print shop or on-line. The cost ranges from $20 to $150 depending on the quality and quantity of cards you order.

An important key to networking is following up. If you meet the best contacts in the world but fail to follow up, they no longer are a contact. Use the note you've written on the back of business cards to help you remember the person and follow up within 48 hours with an email.

Now here is the hard part. What do you say to people whom you don't know? How do you approach the CEO of a company that you adore? Recently, I met with a group of very successful young ladies at a gathering we call "Live Your Best Life". As you know, this phrase came from *O Magazine*. We discussed missed opportunities we have had with potential great contacts because of fear…fear of not knowing what to say, fear of looking like a stalker or just plain crazy. Cynthia Alfaro, the facilitator of this group, decided that we needed practice in order to overcome our fears. So, I volunteered to go first. As I began my introduction, I felt butterflies in my stomach. My friend was standing in front of me, but she was pretending to be Andre Leon Talley, one of my fashion icons. I literally froze. It took about 10 minutes for a meaningful introduction to flow out of my mouth, but after I rehearsed my "speech" and said it out loud, I felt great! This is what we all have to remember: No matter how important a person is in our mind, they are still just a person with fears, feelings, and emotions just like us. My aunt used to tell me, "just ask…the answer can only be yes or no. If you don't ask, the answer will automatically be no." This is a great theory that we can apply to networking.

Helen Walter, CEO of Hamilton Mountain Group Inc., a company that provides "Human Resource (HR) On Demand", services to small and medium sized companies, has provided the following introductions to help you begin the process of connecting.

This student is an intern looking to connect with a mentor before the end of the summer; however, these introductions can be used on any job when you are looking for an advisor, mentor, or person to connect with in management.

"Hi, my name is Sharon. I recently started working at "X" company as a summer intern in the Media Promotions Department. I learned from a colleague that you began your career in media promotions and now manage the entire Promotions Department. I was wondering if I could schedule a half-hour with you to learn more about your career, as I am thinking through what roles I would like to pursue after I graduate from college."

This student is at a career fair and approaches a recruiter at a company he has researched.

Justin: Hi, my name is Justin. I am currently a journalism major at Florida State. I am interested in seeking a full-time opportunity with the NY Times as a journalist. Are you looking to hire full-time journalist?

Recruiter: Yes.

Justin: Well, that's really exciting, I would like to share a copy of my resume and tell you why I would be a great addition to the NY Times company. While at Florida State, I was the editor of the local school newspaper. I earned that role after being a reporter for two years. During that time I covered sports, the arts, school news, etc. I know you have several more people to talk today, but I was hoping to get your card so that I can follow-up with you to discuss full-time opportunities? Thank you for your time and I will be in touch.

This student is introducing herself to her "icon" or your professional hero Dick Parsons, former CEO of AOL Time Warner.

"Hi Mr. Parsons, my name is Sara. I am business major at Rutgers University. I have read several articles about you and your role at Time Warner. It is

truly an honor and a pleasure to meet you. I would like to pursue a career that leads me to become a general manager of a business like Time Warner. I know you are a very busy individual, but I would like to know if you would be available for a half-hour meeting to discuss your career and tips on what it takes to become a leader at a major Fortune 500 company."

Helen's Points to Remember:

- Do research beforehand about the employers at the career fair.
- Employers are very impressed when you are clear and passionate about the type of role you are pursuing.
- Request a business card from the recruiter. In many instances, recruiters will not give out their card and will only be in touch if there is an interest. In this scenario, a student will have to wait to be contacted. If within 2 weeks, the recruiter has not been in touch, it is likely that your resume was not a match for the opportunities they have available.
- Follow up within 1 to 2 days of the career fair while the recruiter still can remember who you are.
- When introducing yourself to a person you don't know, always be prepared to explain why you would like to know that person.

Take the time to practice the introduction speeches above provided by Helen, so that you will be prepared for your next big networking opportunity. Remember that networking is simply connecting with individuals. It is necessary for your career and will be very helpful as you look for a job after college. You will become an expert at connecting with others through practice. I suggest giving it a try today!

The Proof is in the Punchline

Witness #8: Lequite Manning

What is your title?

- Principal - Elementary School

What was your major in college?

- Multidisciplinary School Learning (K-4) and (5-8), a fancy name for Elementary Education

How did you get your current job? Explain your career path.

- I began as a teacher with the Memphis City Schools District in the fall of 2000. I taught for five years. As a teacher, I earned a Master's in Curriculum and Instruction and Ed.S (Education Specialist) in Administration and Supervision. Both degrees were from Union University. I applied and was accepted to be a part of New Leaders for New Schools, a national movement committed to redefining school leadership in 2005. The program provides an accelerated path to leading a school. I served one year as a "Resident Principal". I was appointed principal of an elementary school the following year, 2006, and am currently in this job. This is my 8th year with Memphis City Schools.

What was your first job out of college? How did you get this job?

- Teacher - At a college fair in Chattanooga, I applied to Memphis City Schools (MCS), Shelby County Schools, and Hamilton County Schools (HCS). Both MCS and HCS offered opportunities for employment, but I decided to join MCS. In the summer of 2000 (after graduation) while working for Casual Corner, one of my co-workers told me about a customer who had just walked into the store to shop. I introduced myself to her. She was the assistant principal of a school. I gave her my credentials and sold myself on the sales floor. She invited me to her school for an interview and the rest is history.

Chapter 10

Achieving Your Goals

When traveling to an unfamiliar destination, there are two things you need: 1) To know how long the drive will take. And of course, 2) the directions. To make the journey easier, you may reach out to other resources such as a friend that has traveled there before or an Internet site that gives the best route to take. If the directions are followed, you will eventually find yourself at the destination. Imagine if you jumped into the car and began to drive with no particular destination. There may be many consequences such as: distractions that may cause you to pull over, a car that runs out of gas, or exhaustion may cause you to stop at an unintended destination. College is the vehicle you have chosen to reach a certain destination or goal; therefore, it is important to have a defined destination.

In this chapter we will use your career goals as the destination, but please note that this example can be used for any goal. The first step in setting goals is to establish a long-term goal. A long-term goal is a target you aim to reach over a longer period of time. Once a long-term goal has been established, the next step is to develop short-term goals that will lead to the long-term goal. After you have developed short-term goals, it is time to set a plan in action. I will use my personal goals as an example.

Brandice's Long Term Goal:

To produce fashion shows in every major US city and offer professional exposure to minority designers.

3 Short Term Goals to Reach the Long Term Goal

1) Develop relationships with minority designers and potential sponsors.
2) Produce 1st fashion show in my city as an annual event.
3) Produce a fashion show in another city within a year.

Now that I have a long-term goal and supportive short-term goals, the next step is to put a plan into action. How will I develop relationships with minority designers and potential sponsors? When writing out a clear plan for each short-term goal, set a time limit to each action. For example:

a. Find fashion networking events to attend. Meet designers and follow up. Complete by July 1st.
b. Create a sponsorship package and mail them out to companies.
Complete 1 package per week starting July 10th.

These 2 points could be defined even further by writing out a list of networking events coming up in recent weeks, or I could began to research information on creating a winning sponsorship package. Providing a time frame for each action will help to keep you on track and avoid procrastination.

We will look at a few more examples:

Eric's Long-Term Goal:
To be the VP of Marketing for a Fortune 500 Company
3 Short Term Goals to Reach the Long Term Goal

1) Secure an internship in a marketing department of a company ASAP.
2) Find a mentor in marketing during one of my internships.
3) Interview for at least 5 executive trainee programs.

Example Action Plan for #1

    a. Visit the career center on campus to find information about marketing internships available and the qualifications.
    b. Research marketing internships on career-based websites and note the qualifications needed.
    c. Call local companies and request an information interview to discuss internship opportunities.

The three short-term goals above will definitely get Eric's foot in the door of a company; however, as you can guess, accomplishing only these goals will not secure a position as the VP of marketing. Therefore, the short-term goals will continue to evolve. For example, after Eric has accomplished the three goals above and has a job working as a marketing assistant, the next three goals may be the following:

    1) Be promoted to marketing associate within a year.
    2) Build relationships with at least three individuals in management.
    3) Schedule a lunch with the current VP of marketing to find out his or her career path.

After speaking with the VP of marketing, Eric may learn that he needs to get a master's degree in marketing in order to reach the level of VP. The goals will continue to change until he finally reaches the destination. After the destination has been reached, Eric may decide to establish a new long-term goal.

Goals and plans will change constantly. Changing is not a problem; however, not having a destination is a huge problem. What if you don't have a career goal yet? Well, your destination or goal could be to find a career goal. See the example below:

Long Term Goal:
To find a career interest in order to choose a major
Short Term Goals:
    1) Visit the career center and take an interest assessment test.

2) Research different careers on-line.
3) Shadow at least four professionals in different fields of interest.

Example Action Plan for #1:
- Schedule a meeting with the career center today.

It is now your turn. What is your destination?

My long-term professional goal is to:

_____

_____

_____

How will you reach the destination?
My short-term goals are:

1. _____
   _____

2. _____
   _____

3. _____
   _____

Action Plan

1. _____
   _____
   Deadline for Completion: _____

2. _____
   _____
   Deadline for Completion: _____

3. _____

_____

Deadline for Completion: _____

Limitations

What makes people limit their goals? I believe that the number one reason for limitations is **FEAR**. Is your destination a reflection of your true passion or is it filtered by fear? Did you think about limitations when you set your goal or did you set a goal without limits? If you have written a destination filtered through fear and limits, scratch it out and re-write your goals. Maybe your goal is something that has never been done before in your family, or maybe it is a totally unique idea. That's great! You should not limit your goals based on what has or has not been done before. What if the Wright brothers had not set a goal to fly one day? I'm sure Wright brothers' aspirations were considered ridiculous by many people. What would be different if Frederick Smith, founder of FedEx, had not set a goal to deliver packages overnight? These were ordinary people determined to do extraordinary things, and guess what? They are no different from you!

It would not be fair for me to end this chapter without mentioning the opponent you will face on the road to your destination. The opponent's name is distraction and he comes in many forms including:

- **Time** – If you have not reached your goals in the time you set, it is okay. It is never too late to reach your destination. Once you reach the destination, you will be thankful regardless of the time it took to get there.
- **Failures** – You may experience a flat tire on the journey that slows you down. Fix the tire and get back on the road. Failures are sure to happen. Read the biographies or autobiographies of some of the most successful people in the world, and you will see that failure is merely a lesson to be learned.
- **Comfort** – Do not take your feet off the pedal and cruise. At some point you may have to snap yourself out of a comfort zone and remember that you are on the road to reach a certain destination. Do not stop until you reach the destination.

- **Fear** – We covered your personal fear, but sometimes others can smother you with their own personal fears. It can be tough to loosen the grips of your parents' fears especially because you look to them as a guide for your life. This is officially your road and though you always want to listen to the guidance of your parents, the destination is yours alone.
- **Relationships** – Love for a friend, boyfriend, or girlfriend may cause you to lose view of the destination. Great friends will not take you off the road; they will be the ones to travel the journey with you up the mountains and down the valleys.
- **Setbacks** – You may need to get off the road for a while due to many reasons such as a tragedy, an illness, lack of money, or an unexpected pregnancy. We would hope to never have a setback, but they happen. Life is unpredictable. As you read in overcoming obstacles, it is possible for a family or personal tragedy to occur, but you must remember the destination even though it is perfectly okay to slow down, or even pull over during these moments. During a setback, keep your goals in focus and make a new goal "to get back on the road".

Everyone has faced some form of opposition. So, you must be prepared. The enemy's job is to get you off course from the destination. The great news is that you have a weapon: **FOCUS**. Staying focused on the goal will allow you to combat any move the opponent throws at you. The moment you lose sight of the destination you run the risk of getting lost. Here are a few ways to keep sight of your goals:

Write out your goals and visions and then post them. You could post them on your wall or save them as your screensaver on your computer or cell phone. Whatever your method, just be sure to keep them in sight.

Speak your goals to other people with goals. Sometimes we have big scary goals and visions that we are afraid to share with others for several different reasons. When you speak your goals, it holds you accountable to them. People may not believe in the goals you share, or they may discourage you from moving forward. These are legitimate concerns; however, sharing your goals with like-minded people helps to eliminate most negative feedback.

Create a vision board. A friend of mine has a board on her wall with cut outs from magazines and books that represents the life she wants to live. If you see yourself riding in a Range Rover, cut out a picture and tack it on your vision board. If you want to live in Europe, find pictures and post them. Maybe your goal is to play professional football. Tack pictures of professional teams on your board. Looking at this vision board daily will help to keep you motivated to reach your goals.

You now have the tools to combat any opposition. List your goals, make a plan, and began to implement your weapons to combat the opponent. Anytime you feel defeated, find a book about the life of someone successful, and you will see that they too had great obstacles. Remember, winners always find a way.

The Proof is in the Punchline

Witness #9: Joy Bailey

Who is your current employer?
- A Cultural Consulting Firm.

What is your title?
- Senior Consultant
- Brief Job Description – I work with cultural organizations, like museums, to plan for their futures. A museum director would call her if she/he wanted to expand or build a new facility.

What was your major in college?
- Public Relations
- Master's in Arts Administration

How did you get your current job? Explain your career path.
- I got my current job through networking. I had a classmate that had a job with this firm. She was leaving and wanted to find a good replacement that turned out to be ME.

What was your first job out of college? How did you get this job?
- My first job was in public relations at an African-American museum. I volunteered with the museum during the summers. While still in college, I approached the Director of the museum and said that I could help with PR. At the time, the museum did not have a PR point person or department.

CHAPTER 11

Chapter 11

Creating a Resume

A resume is a snapshot of your professional capabilities. Since many employers receive hundreds of resumes a week, it is important that, after a quick glance, your resume sets you apart from the other applicants. When sending a resume to an employer, personalize it by focusing on the skills and abilities requested for the position you are applying for. As it takes time to create a winning resume, start early. Work with your college's career center as well as other business professional organizations to perfect your resume. Print copies of the final version and request feedback from your advisors and professors.

Avoid making common resume mistakes such as: grammatical errors, resumes that are too long, unfocused resumes, listing references that will not provide a great recommendation, and incorrect contact information. If you are lacking work experience, list your internship and volunteer experiences first. The format is not as important as a clean and neat resume. A neat resume will reflect the same font, preferably 1 inch margins, aligned bullet points, and consistent spacing. Keep semicolons and periods consistent. Words that are in bold and italics should also be consistent. Please see the following for guidance in creating your resume:

Heading

1. Full Name – This should be the name on your birth certificate. Any nicknames can be shared after you are hired for the job, if appropriate.

2. Address – In most cases use your home and/or college address; however, if you are applying for an internship or job in a highly competitive city such as New York, I suggest using the address of where you will live if hired. For example, you may list a family or friend's address. If you use this suggestion, be sure that you have the resources to fly at a moment's notice for an interview. An employer from New York is less likely to choose a person from Tuscaloosa, Alabama over a candidate from New York or surrounding city for an internship opportunity.

3. Phone Number – It is okay to list a home or cell phone number. Employers should be impressed with the voicemail. An appropriate voicemail could start out with "You have reached Kevin Ion. I am currently not available. Please leave a name and number. I will return your call as soon as possible." Music, cursing, or a slang message could cause you to lose a job opportunity.

4. Email Address – The email address provided should be a professional email address such as kevin.ion@gmail.com. Words such as "sexy", "player", or "cutie pie" could quickly land your resume in the "no" pile.

Education

1. University or college you attend
2. The degree that you are pursuing or have obtained
3. Your major and/or minor
4. Expected month and year of graduation
5. Grade Point Average – Only if it is above 3.5

Special Skills

1. Written or Verbal Foreign Language Skills – Being fluent in a foreign language will be impressive to recruiters. If you list fluency or written skills in a foreign language, your skills should be intermediate to advanced.

2. Special Technical Abilities – This should only include special

computer programs that are relative to your industry. For example, Adobe InDesign CS3, would be listed for a graphic design major. Most employers will assume that you already have basic Microsoft Office skills.

3. Sign language abilities

Career Related Experience

1. Internships
2. Career related volunteer experience
3. Study abroad experience
4. Industry related competitions

Work Experience

1. Company name, dates of employment, position held, and location.
2. Accomplishments achieved while on the job - A resume should communicate how well you performed at each job responsibility. For example, if one of your jobs was a sales associate at Sears, your main responsibility could have been to help customers shop. Instead of simply writing this sentence, you want to turn this responsibility into an accomplishment. Try stating that you successfully assisted customers with shopping needs that resulted in a 10% sales increase for the department. Every company wants to know how you would be a benefit to them.
3. Promotions received – Employers want to know if you received a promotion; however, they will not know this fact unless you clearly state it. For example: your resume could say, "promoted from associate to assistant in 5 months."

Honors/Awards

1. List every award or recognition you have received such as Dean's List, Who's Who Among College Students, perfect attendance, etc. List the year the award was received. The

        more awards you list, the more appealing you become to employers.

2. List every scholarship received.

Volunteer Experience – This area should include non-industry related volunteer experience. Any industry related volunteer experience should be listed under "career related experience".

References – This section should be listed on a separate page. Choose references that will give you a great recommendation. Ask a professor, advisor, previous employer, or a leader from one of your volunteer activities for permission to be listed as a reference on your resume. List at least three references. Include the reference's name, company, position, and contact information. When requesting references, it is a great idea to assist the person you are asking by supplying them with a list of your top assets, skills, and achievements.

See the following example:

Christian Woods
christianwoods@thepunchline.com
7914 Dreger Road.
Newark, New Jersey 11111
(222) 222-2222

Education: The University of Tennessee at Martin, Martin, Tennessee
Bachelor of Science
Major: Journalism
Minor: History
Graduation: May 2010
GPA: 3.6

Special Skills: Fluent in French and Spanish

Career Related Experience/Activities:
- August 2008 – present, **Assistant Editor**, College Times. Summarize written material, correct manuscripts, and serve as liaison with the photographers, writers, and designers. Responsible for meeting all deadlines.

- Summer 2008, **Intern**, New York Times. Contributed to two monthly editorials featuring the most recent event information in New York. Assisted with blogs featuring the new "green" campaign.

- Spring 2008, **Competition,** Entered in the "Reporting on the Environment" writing competition sponsored by the Society of Environmental Journalist.

- Fall 2007, **Intern,** The Star Ledger. Assisted the production manager in photo searches, scanned and edited images. Organized and archived files and images.

Work Experience:
File Clerk (May 2007- September 2007 Summer Job)
The Star-Ledger Newspaper, Jersey City, New Jersey

- Created e-file system online for all associate journalists enabling the staff easy and fast access to files.

- Recognized by the associate journalist for exceeding all deadlines for filing and maintaining records neatly.

- Interfaced with department management, lead journalist, and support staff to exchange information; attended and participated in various training opportunities.

Honors/Awards:
University Honor Roll
Who's Who Among American Colleges and Organizations
Jamison Scholarship
Family and Consumer Science Scholarship

Volunteer Experience:
Highway Clean Up (Fall 2007)
Organizer, Diabetes Awareness Program (Fall 2006)
Volunteer, Mothers Healthy Start Program (Fall 2006)
Organizer, Breast Cancer Awareness Program (Fall 2006)
Church Vacation Bible School Teacher (Summer 2005)

References:
Dr. Georgia Byrd
Fashion Merchandising, Professor
340 Timber Hall
Newark, NJ 30000
Phone: (111)-111-1111
Email: gbyrd@aaa.com

Joy Hunter
Manager Banana Republic
1111 N. Germantown Pkwy
Newark, NJ 11111
Phone: (111) 111-1111
Email: jhunter@aaa.com

Tina Lee
CEO, Tina Lee Designs
2393 N. 125th St.
Brooklyn, NY 11111
Phone: (111) 111-1111
Email: tinaleedesigns@aaa.com

In addition to a resume, some employers will require a cover letter. According to Cynthia Alfaro, human resources expert, "A cover letter should be used to connect the dots for the reader. Bullet points should be used to highlight how the qualifications desired in the job posting matches your qualifications. The cover letter is an advertisement of you. I like to start off with quotes as an attention getter; however, this is not required. Think of a cover letter as a networking introduction. This is your sales pitch and the chance to show as much of your personality as possible. The cover letter can also be the way to distinguish you from other candidates."

The following is an example:

Staffing Manager
The New Jersey Chronicles Post
280 Park Avenue
Jersey City, NJ 11111-1111

Dear Staffing Manager:

As journalism major, I have learned about all aspects of the journalism industry including editing, writing, proofing, and designing. In addition to my education, I have received hands-on experience by interning for the New York Times and the Star Ledger. The experience I have received coupled with my education and my enthusiasm for putting my skills into action by working for the New Jersey Chronicles make me the perfect candidate for the assistant editor job. As outlined in the job description, it takes specific skills and experiences to be an effective assistant editor. Below is a brief synopsis of my experiences that illustrate why I will be successful in this role:

1. **Assistant Editor**

    ▪ Two years of editing experience as the assistant editor for the College Times which has a distribution of 70,000 copies. During these 2 years, I successfully interfaced with photographers, writers, and graphic designers.

2. **New York Times Internship**

    ▪ Contributed to monthly editorials and blogs. I successfully built the trust of my peers which was shown evident when I was voted to temporarily fill the position of senior editor for 3 months.

3. **The Star Ledger Internship**

    ▪ Received first hand knowledge of the editing process by attending meetings and shadowing senior editors. Assisted the production manager in photo searches, editing images, and organization of files.

I truly believe my experience is an excellent match for this position and I hope that the above summary, in addition to my resume, can support your similar view.

I look forward to the opportunity to meet with you to further discuss my qualifications, and I am eager to meet with you in person to answer any questions you may have.

Sincerely,

Christian Woods

Follow-Up:

After a resume has been sent to a potential employer follow up is mandatory. Follow-up is the key to receiving feedback. Call the Human Resource Department or the direct contact three to four days after you have sent a resume. Introduce yourself, express your interest, and let them know you recently sent in a resume and would like to know if they've had a chance to review it. Without a follow-up plan your resume may get lost in the stack of resumes employers receive daily. Your dialog may sound similar to this:

> *"Hi Mr. Scott, my name is Brandice Henderson and I read about your Executive Training Program on the Internet. I was*

very excited after I read it. It sounds like a great opportunity. I sent my resume to you last week. Have you had a chance to review it?"

Most likely the answer will be no. If so, continue with the dialogue.

"I understand you've probably been very busy. Would you like for me to email it to you directly?" Wait for an answer and after they have told you to either resend the resume, or they have your resume in hand, you will say, *"I would like to set up a time to speak to you about the program. Do you have an open time on Friday, October 3rd?"* This is going to get the interviewer to actually look on their calendar. Once you receive an answer, say, *"Is morning or afternoon better for you?"*

If that day is not good at all, have another day in mind and ask the same questions. If you suggest a few days and none of these days are working, you should ask the interviewer what day would work best for them. This tactic makes it effortless for a recruiter to give you a chance. Persistence is the key to securing the job in your field of interest.

In many cases, your resume will be the only representation of your abilities. Take the time to invest in your representation by taking resume-writing courses, often visiting the Career Center on campus and requesting the others' feedback. There are also many sources available online that offer resume tips, "do's" and "dont's". Employers will take only a minute or so to scan your resume. This means it must immediately declare, "I would be a great candidate to hire!"

The Proof is in the Punchline

Witness #10: Belle DuChene

Who is your current employer?
- A top 10 men's division at a New York modeling agency

What is your title?
- Jr. Booker – Managing the marketing of models to clients, namely in the fashion industry.

What was your major in college?
- Double Major – French/Textile and Apparel

How did you get your current job? Explain your career path.
- I started out as an intern at a fashion production company for three months. They kept me on as a production assistant for fashion week. During the course of fashion week, two women who had positions above me exited the company and I found myself as the go-to-person in the office. The company was small and I found myself doing things I didn't necessarily want to do. Consequently, I took a leap of faith and resigned. I started sending out resumes. After taking a couple of weeks off, I started temping at a magazine. I didn't like this job either, so I got serious and probably emailed 80 companies. While experiencing my third day in pajamas trying to figure out what I would do in life, I found one last post for a position at a modeling agency. I sent my resume and cover letter, a last ditch effort. My cover letter was very direct. Surprisingly, I got called for an interview. I got the job!

What was your first job out of college? How did you get this job?
- I was determined to get out of Iowa. I sent out personalized cover letters and resumes to every modeling agency and magazine that I could find. I even hand wrote all the envelopes. I landed an internship with a fashion production company that developed into my first full-time fashion job.

Are you happy with your career?
- Of Course! I can see how everything I have experienced has been a part of the final product of having a great job. Even going to France as a foreign exchange student has been a great benefit for me.

What advice would you give a college student concerning finding a job after college, how to choose a major, or any subject related?
- For the most part, I was simply, "Get a degree." In reality, when you get out here, it doesn't necessarily matter what you studied. It's more about what

you've experienced and who you know than a specific degree. I think it is fine to pick a major that is easy for you.

What general life advice would you give a college student?

- Work hard, but play hard. Sometimes when I look back, I think I worked too hard through college. I wish I had had more fun. While grades are very important, I think they can only take you so far. College is an experience. I have learned more under the employment section of my resume than I ever could have under the education section.
- Take your biggest risk after college, because if you fail, you don't have far to fall.
- Build a professional wardrobe.

CHAPTER 12

Chapter 12

ON THE INTERVIEW

The key to mastering an interview is practice. Interviewing can be very intimidating, but if you have practiced the process many times, you will be very comfortable when the real test comes. Fortunately, most employers ask similar questions. This allows you to prepare for the questions in advance. There are several ways to practice. Visit your Career Center to schedule mock interviews, write interview questions and answers, and record yourself asking questions and giving your answers to questions. To find common interview questions and answers visit, the following sites:

- Careerbuilder.com
- Monster.com
- Quintcareers.com
- Hotjobs.com

Common interview questions/inquiries and answers can also be found in relevant articles by typing "common interview questions" into a search engine. Some of the questions that may appear are:

1. Tell me about yourself.
2. Why should we hire you?
3. What is your greatest weakness?
4. Tell me about a time when you overcame an obstacle at work.
5. What is your salary expectation?

The trickiest interview inquiry for me has always been, "Tell about your greatest weaknesses." I don't want to reveal that my actual greatest weakness is that I am sometimes 5 minutes late for work. Who wants to hire someone that's late for work *and* crazy enough to admit it? I learned how to answer this question honestly and intelligently. I discussed weaknesses such as my organization skills. I explain that because it is not my natural ability, I have to go above and beyond what it takes for the person who is naturally organized to insure that I remain organized. The interviewer basically needs to know, "Can you do the job given this weakness?" The answer you give should provide the interviewer with complete assurance that you can. Whatever answer you provide should be turned into a positive. Answering these type of questions will become easier with practice. At the risk of being redundant, again I suggest that you schedule several mock interviews with your Career Center.

After you have prepared for the verbal interview, it is important to understand that there is also a non-verbal interview taking place. **Are you confident?** This isn't a question an interviewer will ask you because the answer is not in your words but in your actions and body language. The following are examples non-verbal communication:

1. **Eye Contact.** Practice looking people in the eyes when speaking to them. If you are not used to making eye contact, this type of communication can be very uncomfortable, but it gets easier with practice. When a prospective employee, or anyone for that matter, cannot look at a person in the eyes, it builds mistrust and does not show confidence.

2. **Handshake.** Giving a firm handshake in an interview speaks volume. Don't shake so hard that you hurt the interviewer's hand, but make it firm. Practice giving a firm handshake to professors, friends, and family.

3. **Smile and Have Energy!** The interviewer will feed off the energy that you provide. If you walk into the interview as if you're walking down the aisle of a funeral, it will be assumed that you are not excited about this opportunity. Smile and show the interviewer that you have personality. Be excited

about the opportunity and the world that awaits you!

4. **Speak Up and Clearly!** I cannot stress the frustration I have with people who speak like they are having a private phone conversation during an interview. Speak out! Don't scream or shout, but your voice should be easily heard and your speech clear. If you have a foreign or distinguishable dialect, slow down and enunciate each word.

5. **Posture, Posture, Posture!** Your posture will reveal a great deal about your confidence whether it is true or not. If you walk in and sit in a chair with your back slumped, the interviewer may question your enthusiasm and self-assurance. Walk into the room with your head up, back straight, and sit down in the same upright position. Practice using good posture so it will not feel uncomfortable. Bad posture = low confidence.

Now that you know how to answer interview questions, both verbally and non-verbally, the next step is to prepare for your outer representation. Your appearance says just as much about you as your verbal communication.

- **Be Well-Groomed.** Check your nails, hair, and face. Your nails should be clean, and if you are wearing nail polish, it should be subtle and neat. Avoid the latest neon colors and stick to clear or neutral polish. Do not ever interview with chipped nail polish. Your hair should be in a conservative style that does not distract from what you are saying to the interviewer. For women, this means a soft ponytail or nice haircut. For men, this means a nice haircut. The face should be neat for both men and women. For men, your face should have a neat shave and for women your makeup should be conservative and nice. When choosing to wear cologne or perfume, go light because you do not know what allergies your interviewer may have. Do not display tattoos or body piercings, as these can be distractions in an interview.
- **Look the Part.** Deciding what to wear depends on the job you are interviewing for. If you're going to a very conservative

company, wear a simple black, navy, or gray suit. If you are interviewing with a hip and trendy company, you may be able to wear a blazer, slacks or a skirt, and a blouse or button down shirt. When choosing your attire keep in mind that you are convincing the interviewer that you can walk into this job tomorrow. Pay attention to details. Small accessories are safe. Make sure your shoes are polished and your heels are not scuffed. To be safe, women should wear closed toe shoes.

- **Wear Confidence.** When you arrive to the interview, your confidence should arrive with you. Communicate, not in a desperate manner, to the interviewer that you want the job and are capable of doing it well. Be sure of yourself, because after all, this employer is interviewing with a great candidate, **YOU**. As an interviewer can sense when someone is not being genuine, be yourself, and stay engaged in the interview. Look intensely at the interview as he/she is explaining the job responsibility. You should also nod your head with understanding.

After the interviewer is finished asking questions, it will be your turn to ask questions. This is your time to show that you have done your homework. Before the interview, research the company and prepare at least five questions relative to the company such as: "I read that your profitability has increased 10% in the past quarter. What factors have accounted for this increase?" or "What is the direction for the new CEO of the company?" Another great question could be focused on the consumer, "I noticed that your ads are now focusing on the Hispanic customer. Is this your new direction?" These types of questions show your intelligence and reflect your interest in the business. In addition to business related questions, ask the interviewer questions about him/herself such as: "How long have you been with the company?" or "What career path did you take to get to your current position?" This gives the interviewer an opportunity to recall some of his/her career accomplishments. This role reversal will put him/her into a positive mindset because you are getting him/her to focus on what he/she has accomplished. Questions and inquiries should also be asked about the company's culture. For example, 'Tell me about the traits and qualities of your most successful employees." or "How would you describe the company's culture?" These questions and inquiries will provide information you will need to decide which company to work for if multiple offers are on the table. You should choose a company to work for, the way you would choose a friend. The personalities should be a good match.

Send a thank you note within 24 hours. In the thank you note include the following points: the time, the topics discussed, the confidence that you have the skills needed to succeed in the job opening, and the excitement that you have about the opportunity.

For Example:

Ms. Jones:

Thank you for meeting with me last Tuesday about the Assistant Copy Editor's position in the Environmental Department. It was great hearing about your experience working with the Jakarta Post during your study abroad program at Yale. The details you provided regarding the skill set needed to perform the job successfully match perfectly with my experience as the Assistant Editor of the College Times. I am excited about the possibility of working as an Assistant Copy Editor. I look forward to hearing from you soon.
Sincerely,
Christian Woods

If you have not gotten a response for the company within a week, call to check up on the status of the position. **Persistence is the key.** If you don't get the job, do not be disappointed. There is something much better waiting for you! Move on to the next opportunity. If you are persistent in sending out your resume and following up with prospective employers, a great job will inevitably appear on the horizon that will be beneficial in the development of your career.

The Proof is in the Punchline

Witness #11: Tamara Wolliston

Who is your current employer?

- A spinal cord injury hospital

What is your title?

- Regional Service Coordinator

What was your major in college?

- Undergraduate: Psychology
- Graduate: Rehabilitation Counseling

Why did you choose this major?

- I had and have a passion to understand and help people. In addition, I was reared, as most people are, in a home with dysfunction. It is often stated that most people go into the psychology field to either help their family or help themselves. My reasoning was both.

How did you get your current job? Explain your career path.

- After completing my undergraduate studies, I pursued the mental health-counseling field. I worked as a call center counselor and as a mental health specialist. While working both positions, I continued my studies and attained my graduate degree. I continued in the field of counseling as a vocational counselor with the State of Georgia. I worked with the State of Georgia for approximately two years. I then applied for a case management position with my current employer for which I was hired. I have now been with the company for over five years and have since been promoted to a regional service coordinator.

What was your first job out of college? How did you get this job?

- My first job out of undergraduate was with Charter Lakeside, a mental health and substance abuse center. I was employed as a call center counselor. I actually found the job through the local Yellow Pages. As an attempt to find an employer, I looked through the Yellow Pages to find companies that provided services in the psychology field. After seeing the ad for Charter Lakeside, I went to their office and completed an application. Ironically, while completing the application, the hiring manager for the position that I was applying for walked past me and asked what position I was applying for. After a brief conversation, he offered me an interview and I was hired.

What advice would you give a college student concerning finding a job after college, how to choose a major, or any subject related?

- I cannot stress this enough, prior to selecting a major, a student should first identify their passion and select a major based on his or passion. Many people choose a major based on what they assume would be most financially rewarding. I do not mitigate the value of financial abundance; however, a wise person once said, "If you love what you do, you will never work a day in your life." For those individuals whose passion in life has not yet been realized prior to entering college or even after beginning college, I would advise them to take advantage of internships. Internships are a great way of exploring various jobs and having a sound understanding of what a job truly entails. In regards to finding a job after college, take advantage of the various resources out there such as the internships, networking, business functions, etc.

What general life advice would you give a college student?

- I would advise any student to follow their passion. Many individuals receive a college degree in one area and end up working in a totally different area. Many factors contribute to this; however, I would guess that a large percentage pursued majors outside their true passion. When you follow your passion, you are more likely to be diligent and tenacious in attaining that vocation. The most important part in following your passion is the likelihood of a person having greater job satisfaction. Job satisfaction is essential to life's satisfaction. They go hand-in-hand.

CHAPTER 13

Chapter 13

The Ten Work Commandments

Once you have been given an opportunity such as an internship, part-time job, or volunteer opportunity, your main objective is to close the deal. Leaving a great impression could lead to a job offer or a job referral. The following ten suggestions are what I call the Ten Work Commandments that will help to ensure that you have a rewarding job experience.

1. **Be Happy**. The road to finding the job of your dreams can be challenging, but the attitude you choose to have along this journey will make all the difference in the way that you and those around you feel. People are drawn to happy and positive people. Also, know that your attitude will sometimes take you further than education and experience.

2. **Be Passionate**. If I have not already stressed it enough, choose a career that you are passionate about. When you have passion and a love for your career, you will be at the top of your game.

3. **Be Assertive**. Remember this is your time to shine. You want your employer to know that you are ready for the next step. Do not get lost in the crowd. Volunteer to assist on projects that are outside of your assigned job parameters and request additional responsibility, if you are not being challenged. The more responsibility you can successfully manage, the more valuable you become to a company.

4. **See Every Task as an Opportunity**. Use every opportunity to shine, no matter how small the task. For example, if you are asked to order lunch, do not view it as a task that is "beneath you". Instead, order lunch and show that you are very detailed-oriented by taking into considerations everyone's tastes (i.e. vegetarian, meat preferences, etc.) when making the order. Simple tasks are your opportunities to shine. It may seem unimportant, but people will want to see that you think strategically on the small issues. A strategic and smart thinker will display these qualities on any task, not just important ones. People are always watching you. Everything you do will be a reflection of your potential.

5. **Be Flexible**. Flexibility is a major plus in any candidate. Be willing to come in extra early or stay late if needed. Do not wait on someone to ask for this commitment, freely give it. Meetings, reports, and presentations may be required from you at the last minute. Your job description may change without warning. If you were hired to answer phones, but you are asked to organize someone's office, order lunch, and run errands, never say, "That's not my job." It disgusts employers to hear those words. Be willing to do whatever it takes to get the job done and always do it with the right attitude. People will take notice.

6. **Be Punctual.** Always arrive for work a few minutes early. Arriving early displays your readiness for whatever the job entails. *Do not come in late under any circumstance.* If you are ever late, due to situations beyond your control, such as a death or severe sickness, **always** call to notify your manager. Traffic jams are never an excuse for being late. Account for traffic jams or other small issues when planning the time it takes to get to work. Also, there is no need to call into work sick unless you have a doctor's note.

7. **Be Focused.** Focus on the task at hand. Take notes, ask good questions, and do your best. Always have a notepad with you to take down notes for everything that you learn. Don't lose focus by turning to distractions such as the Internet, a text message,

or instant messaging. Being distracted could cause you to lose a great opportunity; however, being focused on performing a job well could lead to a full-time position, a promotion, or a referral.

8. **Be Sharp.** Dress and act like a professional. When it comes to professional attire, always dress for the job you want, not the job you have. If you are unsure of the proper dress code, look around you. Pay close attention to how upper management dresses. This will give you a great reference as to what is acceptable in that office culture. If in doubt, wear a blazer. You can never go wrong with a blazer. Pay attention to details such as dirty fingernails, scuffed shoes, dirty pants, or pungent cologne.

9. **Be Approachable and Build Connections.** Connections are essential to successful careers. Do not go into a company being cold and distant. Get to know your peers as well as individuals of both genders in management. Learn the name of every one in management and speak to them by name. These may be people that could refer you to a job, mention your name for a permanent position, or a promotion. Introduce yourself and start a brief conversation. Inquire about your manager's weekend or family pictures on their desks; however, keep the conversation short. You do not want to be the office's "talk-alcoholic". Invite co-workers to lunch to learn about their career paths. Be careful not to join any cliques at work. Take the time to get to know people of all different races and cultures.

10. **Be Ready.** Leave each opportunity by departing with references. These references will be invaluable tools to help you find the next opportunity. Because you have left such a great impression at your job experience, everyone, from your manager to the receptionist, will be happy to provide a reference for you. Ask at least three people if they would write a reference for you. These reference letters will be used when you interview for jobs after graduation. Imagine how impressive it will be for a recent college grad to arrive at an interview with six great references from past employers.

CHAPTER 14

Chapter 14

The Beginning to My End

I first got the idea for this book while speaking with a very frustrated friend. Tamara had just graduated with a master's degree and I with a bachelor's. We were both making less than $27,000 a year and living in Atlanta, Georgia. We both had friends without college degrees who were making (what seemed like) a great deal more money than we were. This only added to our frustration. Neither of us was working a job we liked. I was not even working in a field close to my fashion merchandising major. I was working for a temporary service and she was working as a counselor for the state. While working these temporary assignments and odd jobs, I met many other college graduates in the same situation. They were all just as frustrated as Tamara and I were. I realized that my friend and I were not alone. We were all working jobs in fields that had nothing to do with our passions, goals, or college majors. There were thousands of us college graduates out there with no clue about the punch line.

After several temporary jobs, a construction company finally hired me permanently as an Accounts Payable Clerk. I reluctantly accepted, envisioning my dreams of working in fashion merchandising going down the drain. After three years, two promotions, and a decent salary, the construction company announced it was closing its Atlanta operations. This was my crossroads. Would I accept another job in accounts payable or would I pursue the career of my dreams? I chose the latter, unsure of where to start.

First, I had to go back in time and figure out where I had gone wrong. This mental journey revealed my many mistakes. I realized that I had completed two internships and several volunteer activities but failed to do any networking. Instead of working a job related to fashion merchandising, I chose to work at a beauty supply store every summer. I wanted to become a buyer, yet I had never shadowed or even spoken with a buyer before. I socialized with other students who all looked and talked like me. I never ventured outside of my comfort zone to meet new contacts.

I began looking forward and researched all the jobs and companies I could find relative to my field. The next few months would prove to be a crash course in how to find a job in my major. I conducted research, spoke with Human Resource Managers, and interviewed with several companies, but I received zero job offers. My accounts payable job had ended. I was jobless and my money was quickly depleting. With nothing to lose, I packed my car and moved back to my hometown. What a disappointment! The day I moved back to Memphis, Tennessee and into my parents' house, was one of the worst days of my life. Everyone knew me as the go-getter, so when the go-getter came back home, it was big news. People were talking and it was nothing good. This was one of the most depressing times in my life.

Why was I not prepared for the real world? With my focus being to get my degree, I had worked hard in school. I thought this would be the only thing I needed to secure my professional success. I missed out on opportunities at career fairs. I didn't have the interview skills needed and I failed to build a network. I didn't have a mentor I could call for advice. I didn't even have any experience relevant to my major. At every interview, I was asked about my experience. What did they expect from me? I was only a recent college graduate.

When I moved back to Memphis, I unfortunately climbed back on the "temporary job" track. I thought I was heading in the opposite direction of the career I wanted. But, sometimes opportunities are closer than you know. This is why communication and networking is so important. While working a temporary job, a co-worker informed me that the headquarters for a national clothing store was based in town. I never knew this company even existed. Had I done my research, I could have done internships with this company every summer. My co-worker suggested I send them my resume. I immediately sent my resume and followed up, but I did not receive a call back. After reviewing my resume, my co-worker, who had previously worked in human resources for the United States Military Academy at West Point, made me aware of my many errors. You see, I had only listed my job duties without quantifying my job or communicating the accomplishments I had made. After many revisions, I sent my new resume to the company and received a call back for an interview the same day! A light bulb went on in my head. It all made sense. I had finally discovered the punchline!

I was hired as an allocation analyst. It was not my dream job but my foot was in the door. Never pass up *any* opportunity to get your career started. After a year and a half of learning this job, along with all of the unspoken lessons of a corporate culture, I was promoted to assistant buyer. Six months later, I was promoted to senior assistant buyer, which was equivalent to an associate buyer. I was finally on the right track and was ready to take it a step further.

The job was nice, but my goals were beyond Memphis, Tennessee. My dream was to work in fashion in New York City. I also wanted to attend one of the best fashion schools in the world. I had depleted my savings and had no family or friends in New York City with whom I could crash. I was determined to overcome these obstacles. I had talked about moving to New York for years. People were sick of hearing about it. So many people had counted me out, but while they doubted, I diligently planned.

My time was now or never! While looking for housing and applying for New York's Fashion Institute of Technology (FIT), I began to save money. While planning, I faced many giants. I was rejected for admission at FIT. Other renters immediately grabbed the apartments I found. I received a call that one of my best friends had committed suicide. How would I overcome these obstacles and the tragedy that changed my life forever? I will not say that it was easy to move forward, because it wasn't. With God's help and the support of my family and friends, I pressed forward and coped with these life difficulties. I called and wrote the admissions officer at FIT. I explained that my GPA from undergraduate school was *not* a reflection of my true potential. I was eventually admitted into International Trade and Marketing, a Bachelor of Science degree program. I also found a temporary place to live for two weeks.

After three years of planning, waiting and praying, the day to take the "big step" forward finally appeared on the horizon. With only two pieces of luggage and $1,500, I was on my way to New York City. My newfound networking skills paid off. Through a contact I met in Memphis, I found a job. My new job was at an apparel production company based in New York. My title was Production Coordinator, which entailed managing the apparel production in Indonesia, managing factory capacity, and developing new procedures and processes for our overseas office. I was promoted to assistant production manager after a year and then to production manager a few months later. The title of production manager gave me the responsibility of all the company's apparel production in Sri Lanka, Hong Kong, China, Thailand, Pakistan, and Indonesia. I was responsible for 60 million dollars of business, the production of over 50 million units, and a team of eight employees. This job gave me the opportunity to travel to Jakarta and Bali, Indonesia as well as Dubai. I have had opportunities to meet people from all over the world. In addition to work, my experience at FIT has been outstanding. My current GPA is 3.75. I look forward to graduating with honors.

Although I was performing well as a production manager, I was still not working the job of my passion. I thought that being a buyer was my dream job, but after working in that position, I found that I enjoyed it, but was not passionate about it. I had to find the one thing that I would do even if no one paid me to do it. While attending a fashion show in Brooklyn, I discovered this passion. That show made me think, "Why don't we have fashion shows in my area of New York, Harlem?" Yet, I possessed no resources and knew few contacts. However, I was armed with something so much more powerful than what I did *not* have— passion and determination. Hence, with my mind and heart fully in gear, I immediately began working to produce a first class fashion show in Harlem.

Four months later, "The New Renaissance…Harlem's Fashion Row" fashion show took place. A major fashion show was happening in Harlem and I had coordinated the entire event! The show featured four of Harlem's upscale designers and boutiques. Models included recognized celebrities, as well as other upcoming models from major agencies in the city. The audience included actors, fashion editors, important magazine publishers, well-known fashion photographers, designers, and fashionistas from all over the city. Major fashion publications such as *Women's Wear Daily* and *Style.com* featured the show. That small thought that I birthed in Brooklyn turned into a major production that benefited two non-profit organizations. This was it! My company, Enfiniti Inc., was born. I had found the perfect career. I had discovered my passion!

I traveled a long road to discover the career of my passion. But when you press through the temporary pain you will receive the reward of the lasting gain. My achievements prove it. So, no matter how far you feel you are from reaching your goals, **DO NOT GIVE UP**. It does not matter where you're from or your educational and economic background. You can succeed in anything you put your mind to. Even if you are where I once was, a college graduate not working a job in your field, it is not too late. The road to success starts now. I want to hear your success story. Others need to hear your story.

You now you know the punchline. Use it and let your passion drive you to success.

Brandice Henderson

Acknowledgements

I first want to say thank you to Jesus Christ my savior for His unconditional love and grace. There is nothing I can do without Him, but with Him there are no limits.

To my family who also loves me without conditions, thank you. To my mother and father who have set an example for me on how to do what others think is impossible. Thank you for always believing in me! To my sisters, Tara Lamar and Crystal Oliver—I don't know what I would do without you two. A week without talking to you is like not talking to you forever. I love you both more than you'll ever know. To, Deondra, Joshua, Taijah, Octavious Jr., and Caleb, you all are the loves of my life. Derrick and Octavious I thought I would never have a brother then you two came along. I love you both.

K. Elliott for believing in me and for supporting me. You never let me lose sight of the goal! No matter how many years went by, you continued to keep me focus on this project. Thank you for your guidance throughout this whole project. You are such a wonderful and talented author. I wish to one day have your writing abilities.

This book started as several attempts at writing over the course of 7 years. It was a mess. There was only one person that could organize it into a book: Kersea Johnson. I thank you so much! You are my inspiration and my rock. Who could ask for a better friend? I look at you with your amazing courage to fight Lupus everyday, never giving up. There are so many that need to hear your story of how after being diagnosed with the worst form of Lupus, you worked through the pain to finish your degree. You are truly amazing and one of my biggest heroes. I could not have done this without you. Thank you for ALWAYS for believing in me!

Thank you to Antonio Gipson, who is no longer with us, but who changed my life forever. To the only person who would believe I could actually run for President. You knew no boundaries for my potential and I will never forget you.

To my girls, Katrinna Bryant and Kimberly Galloway, that struggled with me in the last phase of edits. I love you 2 so much! There were days when I knew you put something else aside in your life to care about and attend to my project. I could not have done this without you two. Thank you for your uncensored honesty and a friendship that will last forever.

To Julia Henderson, thank you very much for attending to this book as if it were your baby. I truly appreciate all of your feedback and your kind words on the days that I felt defeated. You will never truly know how much it meant to me to have you be a part of this project.

To my circle of girlfriends who have always believed in me no matter what the situation looks like. I love you girls and you know who you are. I don't know how I could make it without you all. To all of my great friends that continue to amaze me with your love and support I love you all.

Thank you Richard Daniel for your amazing support and push! You have been my angel these last few months and have kept me on task when I started to get sidetracked. You truly have a gift for project management!

To my friends and family that were with me every step of the way during this process thank you! I know I'll get in trouble for this later, but thank you Terrica, Tammy, Darrin, Melvilyn, Dewayne, Troy, Luz, Zayde, Lemar, Rob, Brandy, Yolanda, Vanessa, Leigh, Dalila, Harold, and Jessica. To my LYBL crew, thank you for all of your support! I can't wait to see what life has in store for all of us.

There were so many contributors to this book. Cyndi Alfaro, thank you for you input and expertise with the resume and interviewing chapters. You are such light to all that comes in contact with you. To Helen Walter, you are such an all star! Thank you for taking the time to provide networking quotes and anything else requested from you. Mrs. Bailey, thank you for offering your expertise on the SAT. To Kahmilah Turner, thank you so much for offering your legal services and everything else I needed. Great things are coming your way. Kimberly Dickerson, thank you for doing so many things and the inspiring talks! You are the best! To Kena, thank you for being such an awesome makeup artist. To Kristen Keys, thank you. Dana James thank you for everything! To Alyssa Humphrey my amazing roomie, thank you for helping on the late nights we were up together working on this project. To those of you that were willing to share your stories with me thank you: Erik Pettie, Rashida Maples, Deshawn Nelson, Belle DuChene, Clarence aka Andy Nesbitt, Helen Walter, Jelani Cobb, Joy Bailey, Justin Bird, Kenia Valentin, Lequite Manning, Leslie Waller, Shani Armstrong, Tamara Wolliston, Kimberly Dickerson, and Xenia Murray. I was so inspired by each of you! Gideon thank you for being willing to do the interview, we will take care of you on the next project. Thank you to Dana, Derrick, Deondra, Nikkia and Selwyn for sharing your stories of triumph. Thank you Shawna and Nakea for sharing your publishing expertise. Todd, you have such a wonderful spirit. Thank you for taking a final look at the manuscript and proofing it. To Adolphus Maples you are second to none with your creativity. Thank you for your vision and execution regarding the graphics!

There are so many mentors and icons that have inspired me to fulfill my true potential and follow my dreams. Thank you to B. Oyama, Audrey Smaltz, Lee Reed, Danita King, and Christie Dinham for just being you because it inspires me to be the best me I can be.

Last but not least, to all of the students that have inspired me to share my story and my experiences. Thank you for reaching out to me and I look forward to seeing what life has in store for you!